# MARY BERRY
# FAST CAKES

# MARY BERRY

## FAST CAKES

*Easy Bakes in Minutes*

First published in 2018
by HEADLINE HOME
An imprint of HEADLINE PUBLISHING GROUP
First published as *Fast Cakes* and *More Fast Cakes* in 1981 and 1988 by Piatkus

1

Cataloguing in Publication Data is available from the British Library

Hardback ISBN 9781472243003

eISBN 9781472243010

Commissioning editor: Muna Reyal
Project editor: Jo Roberts-Miller
Recipe consultant: Lucy Young
Design and art direction: Smith & Gilmour
Photography: Georgia Glynn Smith
Food styling: Lisa Harrison and Isla Murray
Food styling assistant: Evie Harbury
Prop styling: Olivia Wardle
Recipe testing: Lucinda McCord and Isla Murray
Printed and bound in China by C&C Offset Printing Co., Ltd.

Headline's policy is to use papers that are natural, renewable and
recyclable products and made from wood grown in sustainable forests.
The logging and manufacturing processes are expected to conform
to the environmental regulations of the country of origin.

HEADLINE PUBLISHING GROUP
An Hachette UK Company
Carmelite House
50 Victoria Embankment
London EC4Y 0DZ

www.headline.co.uk
www.hachette.co.uk

# CONTENTS

Many friends make cakes simply because they love baking – they enjoy making things with their children and grandchildren, and some friends just bake for special occasions – while other friends only bake under duress because they have promised in a moment of madness to provide something for a local fête or school bazaar. When I ask why so many people are put off the idea of making cakes, 'It's such a business!' they tell me. 'All that creaming of butter and sugar. I never seem to have the butter soft enough. And then the tins have to be lined and everything has to be just so. It's all right for you,' they add accusingly, 'you enjoy it!'

Well, so I do. But they are quite wrong if they think that you have to take a whole day off in order to make cakes successfully. Cakes, tea breads and biscuits can all be made quickly and easily with the minimum of fuss and trouble. There is no need to bother with fancy tins or piping bags to produce an informal yet professional finish to all kinds of teatime specialities.

When I sat down to list the different varieties of bake that could conceivably be included in a book on Fast Cakes, I was amazed how quickly I covered the paper. In quite a short time I had written down well over 150 recipe suggestions. Many of them are easy enough even for keen children to make, and I always like to encourage them. Both boys and girls enjoy baking, and are so proud when it comes to presenting the results. And among the recipes included here must be several dozen to tempt even the most reluctant cake-maker!

If you are new to baking, take some time to go through the following pages before you get started. I have included lists of basic equipment, key ingredients for the store cupboard and tips on how to achieve a successful bake every time, among other useful bits and pieces of information. Whatever you do, though, try to have fun with your baking and the end results will be even more enjoyable.

Mary Berry

# BASIC EQUIPMENT

## BAKING TINS

The recipes in this book use one or other of the following tins:

- 2 x 17.5cm (7 in) round sandwich tins
- 2 x 20cm (8 in) round sandwich tins
- 1 x 17.5cm (7 in) deep round cake tin
- 1 x 17.5cm (7 in) shallow square cake tin
- 1 x 20cm (8 in) deep cake tin – round and square
- 1 x 20cm (8 in) loose-bottomed cake or springform tin
- 1 x 20cm (8 in) loose-bottomed, deep, fluted tart tin
- 1 x 23cm (9 in) deep round cake tin (for the Christmas cake)
- 1 x 25cm (10 in) shallow ovenproof dish
- 1 x 900g (2 lb) loaf tin
- 1 x 450g (1 lb) loaf tin
- 1 x 27.5 x 17.5cm (11 x 7 in) baking tin
- 1 x 30 x 23cm (12 x 9 in) traybake tin
- 1 x 33 x 23cm (13 x 9 in) Swiss roll tin
- 6 x 8cm (3 in) loose-bottomed fluted mini tart tins
- 2 shallow bun tins
- 1 deep muffin tin
- 2 large, heavy, flat baking sheets

**ALL MEASUREMENTS GIVEN ARE THE INTERNAL DIMENSIONS** You might find your traybake tin, for example, is listed as 33 x 23cm (13 x 9 in) when the internal dimensions are in fact 30 x 23cm (12 x 9 in). Also, some loaf tins of the same capacity can be different shapes. We use the long variety, rather than the deeper ones that are also available. This won't impact any of the tea bread recipes, for example – your finished bake will just be a bit shorter and deeper than mine – but it may affect a recipe if the loaf tin is lined with one of the ingredients – see page 114 for Mocha Brandy Gâteau.

**MARKING TIN SIZES AND CAPACITIES** Scratch the diameter measurements on the bottom of cake tins and the sizes on the bottom of baking tins – it saves measuring every time. I also write the capacities on the base of porcelain and glass oven dishes with a freezer or ovenproof marker pen – this is such a help when it comes to making a flan and you wonder whether your dish will take a certain amount of liquid.

## COOLING RACKS

When the cakes are cooked, they have to be cooled. It helps, therefore, to have:

- 2 large cooling racks – but you can, of course, always use the grid from your grill pan.

## SMALL BAKE PAPER CASES

Small bake paper cases do vary in size – some are called cupcake cases, others fairy cake cases or simply small cake cases. In order to get around this issue, a general rule to follow is that if you want to ice your small bakes with a glacé icing, make sure you only fill the cases to within 1cm (½ in) from the top of the case. That way, even when the cakes rise there is still some of the edge of the paper case above the cake. It is less important if the cakes are to be uniced, or if you are icing them with a buttercream. If you are making Butterfly Cakes (see page 168), however, it's important to fill the cases to just below the rim so that when they bake they rise above the paper case and give you some cake to slice off and turn into butterfly wings.

For the purposes of our small bakes, we have used three different paper case sizes – muffin cases, fairy cake cases and tiny petit four cases.

Beware of cheap paper cases! Once baked, they come away from the fairy cake or muffin.

## PREPARATION EQUIPMENT FOR A KEEN BAKER

• A selection of oven-safe **glass mixing bowls** that fit inside one another.

• **2 plastic or rubber scrapers – t**his cuts out waste, enabling you to get all the mixture off the sides of the bowls. It makes the children cross, however, because there is not enough mixture left in the bowl for them to lick!

• **1 palette knife** for spreading icing and lifting biscuits off their baking sheets.

• **1 long fish slice** for lifting out slices of cake from roasting tins.

• **1 cake lifter** for moving cakes around safely.

• A set of **measuring spoons** for measuring ingredients such as baking powder or spices – they usually come as ¼ teaspoon, ½ teaspoon, 1 teaspoon and 1 tablespoon. All amounts given in the recipes are for level spoonfuls.

• **1 wire balloon whisk** for beating eggs or small amounts of cream. It gives a light mixture.

• **1 wooden spatula or spoon** – I prefer using a spatula because it is flat on both sides and is easy to scrape clean.

• **Non-stick baking paper** for lining cake tins. Time-saving tip: use a spare moment to cut several circles to fit the tin you use most often and store them in a bag in a drawer, or buy them already cut.

• **Long-life silicone paper** is available in packets or on a roll. It is invaluable for lining the baking sheet when you make meringues or other sugary things as it really is non-stick. Best of all, it can be used time and time again. I just shake off the sugar, fold the paper and put it back in the packet for next time. You can draw circles on it to use as a guide when shaping meringue rings or pavlova, or buy them already cut.

• **Food mixer** – I always use a mixer when making a cake with the all-in-one method. Whether you have a table model or a hand-held mixer, though, follow the instructions provided with your mixer.

• **Food processor** – take care not to over mix! As with a food mixer, it is important to follow the instructions that come with the machine.

## USEFUL STORAGE AIDS AND EQUIPMENT

• **Cling film** is excellent for wrapping cakes because it keeps the moisture in. Its other great advantage is that you can see what it contains! It is also useful for lining tins when making refrigerator cakes – see No-bake Chocolate Juliette on page 113.

• **Kitchen roll** – how did we ever exist without kitchen roll? At one time, cloths and tea towels had to be used for covering and wrapping foods and these needed constant washing and drying so that they could be used again. Kitchen paper is useful for placing between layers of shortbreads etc. in storage tins. It is absorbent and handy for wiping up spills as well.

• **Airtight storage tins** – remember to store cakes and biscuits separately. If you put them together, the biscuits will go soft. Any tins that would rust are best kept in a dry, warm cupboard. Store cake tins one inside the other. Baking sheets and Swiss roll tins are best stored vertically between two divisions, as you would store tea trays.

• **Polythene boxes** with clips to close are useful in various sizes to fit cakes or bakes.

# PREPARATION METHODS

All-in-one means exactly what it says. Everything goes into the same container at once – either into a bowl for mixing with an electric food mixer, or into a large saucepan for mixing by melting (for example, the Honey Cake on page 90). Apart from the speed of preparation, this also cuts down on the washing up.

Do follow the recipes carefully and use both self-raising flour and a little baking powder for the all-in-one method. Mixing in this way is far quicker than in traditional cake-making, so there is not enough air beaten into the mixture to make it rise using flour alone. You need the baking powder to give the extra lift. But do stick to the amount of baking powder given in the recipe – if you use too much, the cake will rise quickly when it first goes into the oven and then flop down before it is properly cooked.

A food mixer is perfect for all-in-one mixtures – my own is in constant use – but do take care not to over mix. Check through your instruction book for any special tips. I often put more mixture than I really should into my free-standing mixer. I prevent the flour from showering all over the floor by carefully covering the front end of the machine and the bowl with a tea towel. If you do the same, remember to stand by the machine while it is mixing to be sure that the tea towel does not accidentally slip into the mixture and get caught up in the spindle!

## HOW MUCH MIXTURE A CAKE TIN TAKES

• 2 x 17.5cm (7 in) sandwich tins take 450g (1 lb) at 180°C/Fan 160°C/Gas 4 and need about 25 to 30 minutes cooking time.

• 2 x 20cm (8 in) sandwich tins take 675g (1½ lb) at 180°C/Fan 160°C/Gas 4 and need about 35 minutes cooking time.

• 18 small cakes take 450g (1 lb) at 200°C/Fan 180°C/Gas 6 and need about 15 minutes cooking time.

• 1 x 17.5cm (7 in) round cake tin takes 1.1kg (2½ lb) at 160°C/Fan 140°C/Gas 3 for about 1½ hours for a fruit cake.

• 1 x 20cm (8 in) round cake tin takes 1.7kg (3¾ lb) at 160°C/Fan 140°C/Gas 3 and needs about 2½ hours for a fruit cake.

• 1 x 17.5cm (7 in) square tin as for a 20cm (8 in) round tin.

## HOW MUCH MIXTURE A CAKE TIN TAKES WITH WHISKED CAKES

• 2 x 17.5cm (7 in) sandwich tins take a 3-egg mix. Bake at 190°C/Fan 170°C/Gas 5 for about 20 minutes.

• 2 x 20cm (8 in) sandwich tins take a 4-egg mix. Bake at 190°C/Fan 170°C/Gas 5 for about 25 minutes.

• 1 x 32.5 x 22.5cm (13 x 9 in) Swiss roll tin takes a 3-egg mix. Bake at 220°C/Fan 200°C/Gas 7 for about 10 minutes.

# TIPS FOR SUCCESS EVERY TIME

1 *Choose a recipe that is going to be popular with the family.* If you know it is all going to be eaten on the day it is made you can choose one that wouldn't keep, such as Just Rock Cakes (see page 185) or Classic Special Scones (see page 298). If you want it to last for some time in the cake tin choose a rich one like the Vicarage Fruit Cake (see page 146). If you know that one of your family or friends loathes coconut, ginger or banana then obviously avoid these flavours! Of all the recipes I have included, some, I must admit, are more popular with my family than others. If it's any help to you, these are the ones we enjoy most and which have become my stand-bys:

**FOR EVERYDAY**
Just Rock Cakes
Mincemeat Cake
Fruit Malt Loaf
Classic Special Scones
Proper Shortbread
Fairings
Botermoppen
Easy Apple Cake
Lemon Drizzle Traybake

**FOR SPECIAL OCCASIONS**
Coffee Fudge Traybake
Superb Carrot Cake
Fresh Raspberry Cream Pavlova
Special Apricot Cake
Brandy Snaps
No-bake Chocolate Juliette
Tacky Gingerbread
Summer Raspberry Shortbread
Victoriana Christmas Cake
Chocolate Éclairs

**WITH CHILDREN IN MIND**
Millionaire's Shortbread
Annabel's Caramel Bars
Caroline's Chocolate Slab
Sultana Flapjacks
Simple Chocolate Cake with Fudge Icing
Chocolate Cream Fingers
Iced Shape Biscuits

2 *Check that you have time to make the recipe and bake it before starting.* To help I have put the preparation and baking times. Remember, though, that your preparation time could be longer if you have to chop the almonds or defrost some cream from the freezer to fill a sponge. If you have to nip out and see a neighbour, select a recipe that uses the all-in-one method. The mixture can be prepared and put in the tins ready for baking when you return. They seem to rise just as well. The uncooked mixture will not spoil if, as so often happens with me, the ten minutes you thought you would be away turns into half an hour. Cakes already in the oven are not so accommodating!

I have found that you can split the preparation and baking of other recipes, such as fruit cakes, teabreads and shortbread type biscuits. Very often I prepare the mixture for all-in-one Victoria sandwiches and then find that I have an unexpectedly long phone call and there is no time to bake them before, say, fetching the children from school. I simply put the mixture in the tins and then bake them when I get back. Biscuits and shortbread can in fact improve by being left to chill in the fridge before baking. Recipes that you must prepare and then bake straightaway are whisked sponges, meringues and any recipes with beaten egg whites folded in at the end of the recipe.

**3** *Make sure you have everything you need before you start baking*: the cake tin or tins and all the ingredients. And don't improvise with ingredients unless you've tried the recipe at least once before! Gather the ingredients together, weighing them carefully and ticking the items off in pencil, if you like. This way you won't forget to add the sugar! Time can be saved by weighing the ingredients straight into the mixing bowl. Incidentally, I have deliberately left salt out of most of the recipes. I find it makes no difference to the flavour and using it means one more thing to remember!

**4** *Make sure you read the recipe properly!* It's very important to do this, even though you may feel you know the method.

**5** *Mixing the recipe.* I have tried to use the all-in-one method whenever possible because it is fast and effective. Take a large roomy bowl, put in all the ingredients and beat with an electric mixer until well blended. I find it a marvellously sound way of mixing and I would never go back to the traditional method. If you prefer to use butter instead of baking spread then allow it to become soft and creamy before adding it. Take care not to get it too warm because the butter will be an oily consistency.

**6** *Follow the method conscientiously.* I don't believe you will think of a short cut I haven't already tried! The method I give for each recipe is one which, from experience, I find works best. So, if you are the sort of person who likes to experiment, may I respectfully suggest you wait until you've had a go doing it my way first!

**7** *Mixing with an electric mixer saves considerable time.* I use both a free-standing and a hand-held mixer constantly. If you're canny and plan a baking morning, you can start by rubbing in fat to flour for pastry, then make a plain cake then a chocolate cake without washing up the mixer in between! I find using an electric mixer best for all-in-one cakes. If using a free-standing mixer beat for 1 minute or for a hand-held mixer 2 minutes. When adding dried fruit, it is often best to do this by hand or to just mix for a few seconds as the fruit could easily be chopped up which would spoil the mixture. You can, of course, beat by hand but that will take a little longer. Food processors are marvellous for making pastry, chopping nuts and rubbing mixtures, too.

**8** *Prepare your tins.* To save time in the long run, use non-stick paper or long-life silicone paper to line baking sheets. When biscuits are cooked, they slide off easily. With experience, you will soon find that sometimes you can just grease the baking sheet, for example when baking scones. You will know whether your own cake tins stick or not, but I prefer to buy loose-bottomed round cake and sandwich tins or to line an ordinary cake tin with non-stick baking paper. It is maddening to have a cake stick to a tin, so I consider it well worth bothering to take care and line them first. Be sure to prepare well the baking sheets for meringues and sugary items that really stick. I recommend lining the baking sheets with long-life silicone paper or non-stick baking paper.

9 *The temperature of the oven is most important when baking.* If you are not absolutely certain that your oven temperature is correct, beg, borrow or buy an oven thermometer and carry out a check yourself. Buying a thermometer is cheaper than asking a utility engineer to visit your home and test your thermostat. Alternatively, if in practice you notice that your cakes always take a longer or shorter time to cook than is given in the recipe, adjust the oven setting accordingly next time and make a note of it. And never open the oven door during the early part of the baking time or move the cake tin in the oven. Both actions will make the cake sink in the middle.

**USING CONVENTIONAL GAS OR ELECTRIC OVEN** If only one item is being baked, bake on the centre shelf. If baking two, either put both on the same shelf, or consult the manufacturers' cookery book as to shelf positions.

**USING FAN OVEN OR FAN-ASSISTED OVEN** The baking times and temperatures differ from the conventional ovens so do consult the manufacturers' cookery book and take their advice. Usually, you need to decrease the baking temperature by 20°C. For example, something like a Victoria sandwich bakes at 180°C in a conventional oven and 160°C in a fan oven.

**USING A MICROWAVE OVEN** Consult the manufacturers' cookery book for baking methods and times. It is difficult to give advice generally as the electrical output of the different makes and models of microwaves varies. Microwave ovens certainly speed up the baking time but unless the cake is flavoured with chocolate or coffee the appearance is a little pale and disappointing. However, this can be overcome by icing or frosting the cake. Cakes must be baked in non-metallic containers.

**BAKING SEVERAL CAKES IN ONE GO ON DIFFERENT SHELVES** Even though modern ovens are thermostatically controlled, I find that if several items are baked at once they take longer to cook and in the case of a three-tier wedding cake it can lengthen the time by an hour or so. Keep an eye on them during the latter part of the baking and, lifting them carefully without banging, move the tins or baking sheets around so that each batch is evenly browned. Forgetful cooks would be well advised to use a pinger-timer to remind them to check. The timer, of course, should be set to go off at a shorter interval than the baking time in the recipe.

# CHOOSING, USING AND STORING YOUR CAKE INGREDIENTS

Store your cake ingredients in a dry cupboard in logical sections, keeping the various flours, sugars and fruits together. Leave the flours in the bags they come in, and the sugars as well, unless you wish to decant the ones you use most, like caster sugar. I also keep a separate jar of caster sugar with added vanilla pods so that I always have vanilla sugar on hand for flavouring. If you buy goods in bulk, such as 3kg (7 lb) bags of dried fruit or large bags of flaked almonds, keep small amounts in the store cupboard and freeze the remainder in polythene bags for up to a couple of years.

**FLOUR** I always use a good-quality flour and in most cases the self-raising variety. Many of my recipes also use additional baking powder. Some recipes use wholemeal or granary flour, but these usually replace only half of the white, so that the finished cake is not heavy (which would be the result of using all brown wholemeal flour). Brown wholemeal flour is more nutritious than white because it is less refined, and it gives us more fibre, which is recommended for good health. However, it does absorb more water or liquid than white flour, so more liquid is added in these recipes and extra baking powder is also added to make them rise sufficiently.

**SUGAR** In these recipes I have mostly used unrefined or natural sugars wherever possible. Unrefined demerara sugar is clearly labelled, and the muscovado sugars are both completely natural and have an excellent flavour. If necessary, light and dark soft brown sugars can be substituted for the respective muscovado sugars, but I find there is a loss of flavour.

It is essential to store all sugars in dry conditions, and icing sugar should always be sifted before use. Remember when using golden syrup or treacle not to be over-generous, as this can upset the balance of ingredients and alter the results of a recipe considerably.

**EGGS** All of the recipes use size 2 eggs (large 50g/2 oz) which give good results. I always find the best results are from eggs that have been left out of the fridge a little while before using them, so that they are at room temperature.

**FATS AND OILS** I prefer to use a high-fat baking spread instead of butter for most of my cakes. Spread for baking simplifies the making process because you do not have to remove it from the refrigerator and give it time to soften before you use it. In fact, it is important to use spread straight from the refrigerator. If it is too soft, the results are not as good. I use butter where the flavour is important, though, for example in Chewy Almond Flapjacks (see page 266) or in Traditional Dutch Butter Biscuits (see page 209) where the buttery flavour is essential. I use sunflower oil in recipes that need oil, as it is light and has little flavour.

**FRUIT** It is not necessary to wash dried fruit now, as this is done before packaging and sale to the public. Always buy dried apricot pieces to use in a cake, as they will be cheaper than whole dried ones and it will also save the time that is taken up by chopping. Glacé cherries usually have a well of syrup in the centre, so it is better to cut them in half or quarters and wash and dry them; this will prevent the fruit sinking in a cake.

**SPICES** It is important for ground spices to be kept dry and ideally in the dark, as they fade in sunlight. They should be replaced yearly as they tend to lose their flavour and potency.

**NUTS** If a recipe calls for chopped nuts, it is practical to buy broken or pieces of nut rather than whole ones: this not only saves money but time as well. Store nuts in separate bags for the different types in your freezer. In a store cupboard in a warm kitchen, nuts may go off quickly as the fat in them can turn rancid.

**LEMONS** I always use unwaxed lemons. If you use the waxed variety the zest will not have the best flavour. Warm lemons for a few minutes in a microwave to extract the maximum juice.

**CHOCOLATE** The strongest and most economical way of adding chocolate flavour is to use cocoa powder. If a recipe calls for melted chocolate, I have always used plain Bournville, as it is available at the corner shop.

**COFFEE** Coffee essence gives a good coffee flavour and, being a liquid, is easy to mix. However, if this is not available, instant coffee mixed with a little hot water and then added gives quite satisfactory results. Otherwise, you can use very strong proper coffee.

# ONCE YOUR CAKE IS BAKED

## HOW TO KNOW WHEN A CAKE IS DONE

There is no great mystery to baking a cake. It is done when it looks and smells ready. In most cases, the principal signs are when the cake shrinks slightly from the sides of the tin and when the top of the cake springs back after being pressed lightly with a finger.

Large fruit cakes need a further test. Simply push a fine metal skewer into the centre of the cake and if it comes out clean and shiny, the cake is ready. If the skewer has some cake mixture clinging to it, cook for a few minutes longer, checking again from time to time. Sometimes, the cake is not quite done in the middle but the top is getting brown and the currants on the surface seem to be burning. In this case, place a piece of foil lightly on the top, lower the temperature and leave to cook for a bit longer.

## HOW TO KNOW WHEN BISCUITS ARE DONE

With biscuits and shortbread, test by eye, checking that the colour is right. As a general rule biscuits should be turning a gentle caramel brown colour at the edges. Naturally chocolate-flavoured items will be a darker colour at the edges, not only on the top but underneath as well. It is sometimes difficult to tell when a thick shortbread is ready just by looking at the top, so I take the tin from the oven and lift a slice carefully out from the centre. The underneath should be very pale golden brown and the middle of the underside should look short and cooked, not close and soggy.

Biscuits on the outside of the sheet may bake more quickly than those in the middle. In this case, remove them to a wire rack and return the rest to the oven for a few more minutes.

## COOLING BISCUITS

Remove from the oven, leave on the baking sheet to firm a little then slip a palette knife under them and remove to cool on a wire rack.

Store in an airtight tin with kitchen paper between the layers.

## COOLING CAKES

Leave cakes in the tin to cool for a while before turning them out on to a wire rack (10 minutes for a sponge sandwich, 30 minutes for a large cake, or see individual recipes). In order to turn the cake out quickly without breaking it, run a knife round the edge of the tin before inverting the tin. If the tin has been lined, turn upside down on to a folded tea towel, take away the tin, peel off the paper and transfer the cake to the cooling rack.

With all-in-one Victoria sandwiches, I turn out the sponges on to a wire rack and then replace the tins over them. This prevents the moisture from evaporating while the cakes are cooling and it does not make the sponges soggy.

Store cakes in an airtight tin once cool.

## FREEZING BISCUITS

There is little point in freezing biscuits as most of them keep for a couple of weeks in a tin. However, they can be stored in the freezer for up to 3 months if required.

Raw shortbread type of biscuits can be rolled into sausage shapes, wrapped in cling film and frozen. When slightly thawed, slices can be cut from the sausages and baked freshly as needed.

Incidentally, there is no need to freeze meringues, but you can if you wish.

## FREEZING CAKES

All cakes freeze extremely well, except for those containing breakfast cereal, like cornflakes or Rice Krispies. Freeze them as soon as they are cool. If not iced or frosted, wrap them carefully in cling film or put in a polythene box. If iced or frosted, freeze uncovered until solid then wrap carefully and label and return to the freezer to freeze solid. I try not to keep cakes in the freezer longer than three months, as those kept longer seem to lose a little of their flavour.

Fruit cakes and shortbreads, however, can stay in the freezer for many months, where I find they mature well. You may well ask why bother to freeze them at all, as they keep well in an airtight tin in a cool, dry storage cupboard. Well, frankly, most kitchens are too warm for ideal storage conditions and some have insufficient room.

The freezer not only maintains the cakes in good condition but it is also a deterrent to thieving fingers! The family is unlikely to raid the freezer but a cake in a tin is an open invitation!

# HELP! IT HAS ALL GONE WRONG

Frankly, I don't think anything should go wrong but just in case you
do have the occasional failure, here is a guide to the possible reasons:

## ALL-IN-ONE MIXTURES

| | |
|---|---|
| **Coarse texture** | Too much baking powder |
| **Collar edge on cake** | Rising of cake was too rapid and it then sank. One of two causes: either the cake was placed on too high a shelf in the oven, or there was too much baking powder in the mixture |
| **Damp, close texture** | Cake was removed from the oven too soon |
| **Domed, cracked top** | Oven too hot or cake placed too high in oven |
| **Hollow top** | Mixture beaten too long; too slow an oven; cooking time too short; spread for baking allowed to become oily during very hot weather |
| **Pale in colour although fully cooked** | Oven too cool or cake placed on too low a shelf |

## MELTED MIXTURES

| | |
|---|---|
| **Cracked top** | Too much baking powder, syrup or treacle; too hot an oven, door opened too early |
| **Doughy texture** | Too much flour or baking powder, not enough liquid |
| **Hard on outside** | Too much liquid or syrup; oven too hot |

## WHISKED MIXTURES

| | |
|---|---|
| **Specks of uncooked flour** | Poor whisking; flour not mixed in properly |
| **Sticky, damp texture when cold, sticking to sides of tin** | Usually caused by being in too much of a hurry and skimping each stage; ingredients not correctly measured; under-whisking so the sugar has not properly dissolved; under-baking; tin badly prepared. Any or all of these will give sticky results |
| **Too shallow, not risen** | Insufficient whisking; too cool an oven; not enough baking powder |
| **Uneven rising** | Flour not folded in properly; oven shelves not level; mixture unevenly distributed in the tin before baking |
| **Wrinkled top to cake** | Under-baking; tin too small |

# EVERYDAY CAKES

# ALL-IN-ONE VICTORIA SANDWICH

*I no longer prepare a Victoria sandwich with the traditional creaming and folding methods, as this all-in-one method gives excellent results every time. Make sure to use the baking spread straight from the fridge – you don't want it too soft.*

**SERVES 8**

225g (8 oz) baking spread, from fridge

225g (8 oz) caster sugar, plus extra to sprinkle

4 large eggs

225g (8 oz) self-raising flour

1 level tsp baking powder

200ml (7 fl oz) double cream

about 6–8 tbsp strawberry jam

**1** Preheat the oven to 180°C/Fan 160°C/Gas 4. Grease two 20cm (8 in) round sandwich tins and line the bases with non-stick baking paper.

**2** Measure the baking spread, sugar, eggs, flour and baking powder into a large mixing bowl and beat with an electric mixer until well blended and smooth.

**3** Divide the mixture between the tins, level out evenly and bake in the preheated oven for about 25–30 minutes, or until well risen and the tops of the sponges spring back when lightly pressed with a finger.

**4** Leave to cool in the tins for a few minutes then turn out, remove the paper and finish cooling on a wire rack.

**5** To make the filling, measure the cream into a large bowl and whisk until stiff.

**6** When completely cold, sandwich the cakes together with the jam and cream. Lift on to a serving plate and sprinkle with caster sugar.

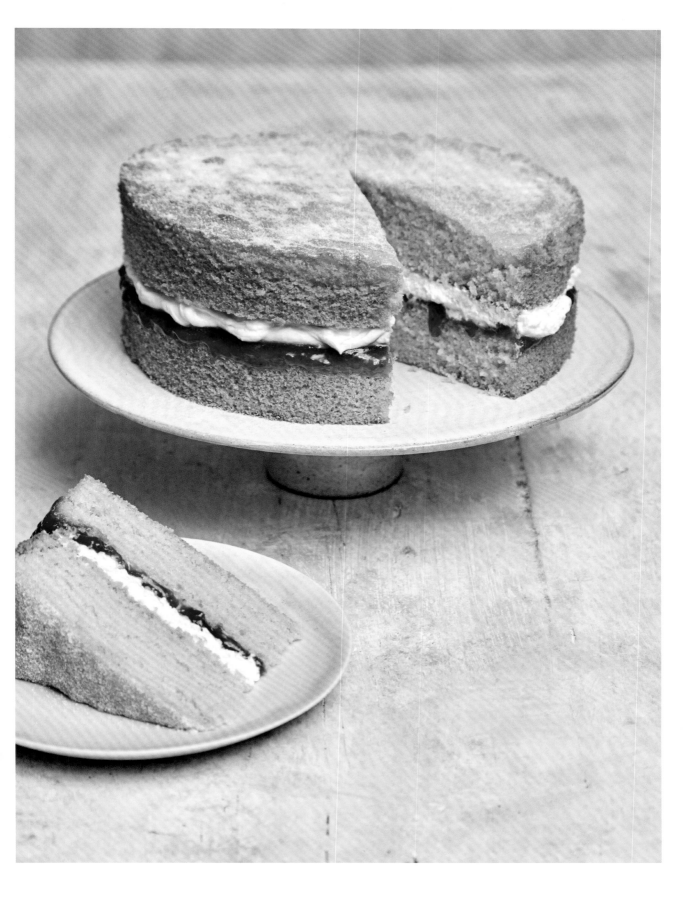

# LEMON SPONGE SANDWICH

*If you can find orange curd, you could make this sponge sandwich with orange zest in place of the lemon and use orange curd as the filling.*

**SERVES 8**

225g (8 oz) baking spread, from fridge
225g (8 oz) caster sugar, plus extra to sprinkle
4 large eggs
225g (8 oz) self-raising flour
1 level tsp baking powder
finely grated zest of 1 lemon
about 6 tbsp lemon curd

**1** Preheat the oven to 180°C/Fan 160°C/Gas 4. Grease two 20cm (8 in) round sandwich tins and line the bases with non-stick baking paper.

**2** Measure the baking spread, sugar, eggs, flour, baking powder and lemon zest into a large mixing bowl and beat with an electric mixer until well blended and smooth.

**3** Divide the mixture between the tins, level out evenly and bake in the preheated oven for about 25–30 minutes, or until well risen and the tops of the sponges spring back when lightly pressed with a finger.

**4** Leave to cool in the tins for a few minutes then turn out, remove the paper and finish cooling on a wire rack.

**5** When completely cold, sandwich the cakes together with the curd. Lift on to a serving plate and sprinkle with caster sugar.

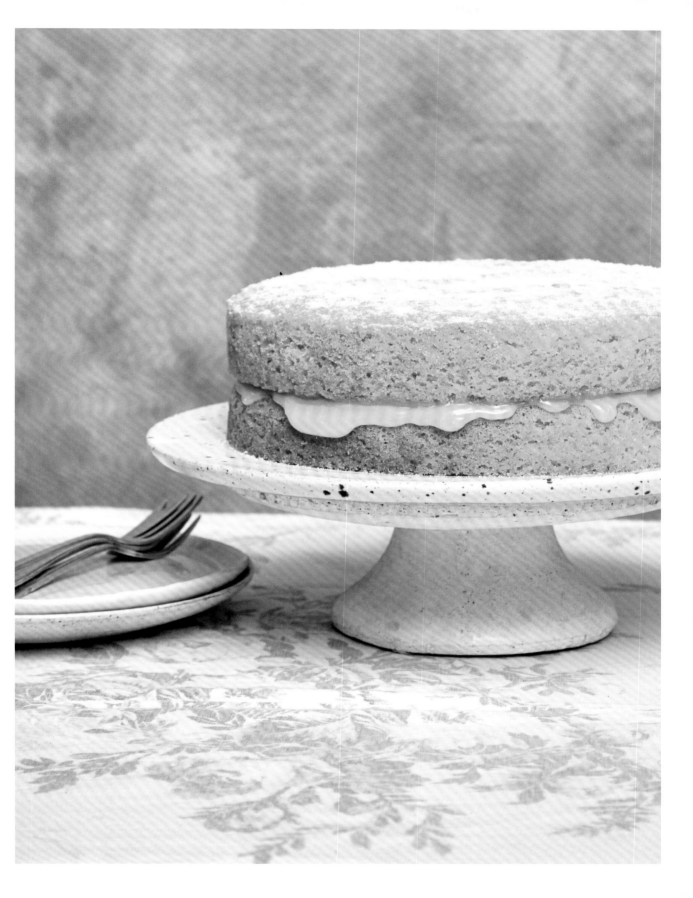

# COFFEE SPONGE SANDWICH

*A lovely change to a classic Victoria sponge.*

**SERVES 8**
2 heaped tsp instant
    coffee granules
225g (8 oz) baking
    spread, from fridge
225g (8 oz) caster sugar
225g (8 oz) self-raising
    flour
4 large eggs
1 level tsp baking
    powder

*For the icing*
75g (3 oz) butter,
    softened
225g (8 oz) icing sugar,
    sifted, plus extra
    to dredge
1 tbsp coffee essence

**1** Preheat the oven to 180°C/Fan 160°C/Gas 4. Grease two 20cm (8 in) round sandwich tins and line the bases with non-stick baking paper.

**2** Dissolve the instant coffee in 1 tablespoon of boiling water and mix until smooth.

**3** Measure the baking spread, sugar, flour, eggs and baking powder into a large mixing bowl. Add the coffee mixture and beat with an electric mixer until well blended and smooth.

**4** Divide the mixture between the tins, level out evenly and bake in the preheated oven for about 25–30 minutes, or until well risen and the tops of the sponges spring back when lightly pressed with a finger.

**5** Leave to cool in the tins for a few minutes then turn out, remove the paper and finish cooling on a wire rack.

**6** To make the icing, blend the butter with the icing sugar and coffee essence.

**7** When the cakes are completely cold, sandwich them together with the icing and lift on to a serving plate. Dredge with a little icing sugar before serving.

# MADEIRA CAKE

*A classic cake. Use soft butter for an even better flavour.*

**SERVES 6**

225g (8 oz) self-raising
  flour
175g (6 oz) butter,
  softened
175g (6 oz) caster sugar
finely grated zest of
  1 lemon
50g (2 oz) ground
  almonds
4 large eggs
3 slices candied peel,
  to garnish (optional)

1 Preheat the oven to 180°C/Fan 160°C/Gas 4. Grease a 17.5cm (7 in) deep cake tin and line the base with non-stick baking paper.

2 Measure all the ingredients into a large mixing bowl and beat with an electric mixer until well blended and smooth.

3 Turn the mixture into the tin, level the top and bake in the preheated oven for about 55–60 minutes. A skewer inserted into the centre of the cake should come out clean. If liked, place 3 slices of citron peel on top of the cake after the first 30 minutes of cooking time.

4 Leave to cool in the tin for 15 minutes then turn out and finish cooling on a wire rack.

5 Store in an airtight tin.

# COFFEE WALNUT GÂTEAU

*If there is a lot left over, then store slices in the freezer for up to 3 months.*

**SERVES 8**

1 level tbsp instant coffee granules
175g (6 oz) baking spread, from fridge
175g (6 oz) caster sugar
3 large eggs
175g (6 oz) self-raising flour
1 level tsp baking powder
50g (2 oz) walnuts, chopped

*For the icing*
75g (3 oz) butter, softened
225g (8 oz) icing sugar, sifted
1 tbsp milk
1 tbsp coffee essence

*For the decoration*
10 walnut halves

**1** Preheat the oven to 180°C/Fan 160°C/Gas 4. Grease two 20cm (8 in) round sandwich tins and line the bases with non-stick baking paper.

**2** Dissolve the instant coffee in 1 tablespoon of boiling water and mix until smooth.

**3** Measure all the ingredients for the cake into a large mixing bowl and beat with an electric mixer until well blended and smooth.

**4** Divide the mixture between the tins, level out evenly and bake in the preheated oven for about 25–30 minutes, or until well risen and the tops of the cakes spring back when lightly pressed with a finger.

**5** Leave to cool in the tins for about 5 minutes then turn out, remove the paper and finish cooling on a wire rack.

**6** To make the icing, cream the butter and icing sugar until smooth, then stir in the milk and coffee essence.

**7** Sandwich the two cakes together with one-third of the icing. Spread the remainder over the top and sides of the cake and decorate with the walnut halves.

# MARBLE CAKE

*Children love this cake and it is not difficult to make and looks good when cut. Ice it as you like – try the chocolate icing on page 96 – or serve it plain, sprinkled with icing or caster sugar.*

**SERVES 8**

175g (6 oz) baking spread, from fridge
175g (6 oz) caster sugar
175g (6 oz) self-raising flour
1 level tsp baking powder
3 large eggs
1 level tbsp cocoa powder
1 tbsp hot water
a few drops red colouring

**1** Preheat the oven to 180°C/Fan 160°C/Gas 4. Grease a 20cm (8 in) deep cake tin and line with non-stick baking paper.

**2** Measure the spread, sugar, flour, baking powder and eggs into a large mixing bowl and beat with an electric mixer until well blended and smooth.

**3** Measure the cocoa into another bowl with the water and stir thoroughly until blended and smooth. Add a third of the sponge mixture to this and mix together.

**4** Put half of the remaining sponge mixture in a third bowl and colour it pink with the red colouring.

**5** Choose one of the mixtures and place tablespoons of this at regular intervals around the tin. Fill the gaps with the two other contrasting colours until all the mixture has been used. The cake will find its own level as it bakes so there is no need to smooth the top. Bake in the preheated oven for about 40–45 minutes, or until golden brown, well risen and the top of the sponge springs back when lightly pressed with a finger.

**6** Turn out and leave to cool on a wire rack. Ice or decorate as required.

# FRESH CREAM SPONGE CAKE

*This sponge cake – topped with sprigs of mint and a few pretty flowerheads – is perfect to serve in the summer for tea. If you like, mix 100g (4 oz) fresh raspberries with the cream for a real treat. The sponge bases freeze well and can be frozen ahead then brought out of the freezer, thawed and filled when required.*

**SERVES 8**

4 large eggs
100g (4 oz) caster sugar
100g (4 oz) self-raising
 flour

*For the filling*
about 6–8 tbsp
 raspberry jam
300ml (½ pint) double
 cream, whipped
100g (4 oz) fresh
 raspberries, hulled

*For the decoration*
a little sifted icing sugar
a sprig of fresh mint
small flowerheads
 (optional)

**1** Preheat the oven to 180°C/Fan 160°C/Gas 4. Grease two 20cm (8 in) round sandwich tins and line with non-stick baking paper.

**2** Break the eggs into a warmed bowl and whisk in the sugar until the mixture is light and creamy and leaves a trail when the whisk is lifted out.

**3** Sift in the flour and very carefully fold it in with a metal spoon.

**4** Divide the mixture between the tins, level out evenly and bake in the preheated oven for about 20–25 minutes, or until well risen and the tops of the sponges spring back when lightly pressed with a finger.

**5** Turn out and leave to cool on a wire rack.

**6** Spread one half of the cake with raspberry jam. Top with the whipped cream and scatter with the fresh raspberries. Sandwich the other cake on top, dust lightly with icing sugar and decorate with a sprig of fresh mint and a flower, if liked, to serve.

# SPECIAL LEMON CAKE

*The lemon cream filling makes this sponge really rather special. It is at its best if you use home-made lemon curd. This is a fatless sponge but the cream makes it extra special.*

**SERVES 8**

4 large eggs
100g (4 oz) caster sugar
100g (4 oz) self-raising flour
200ml (7 fl oz) double cream
6 tbsp luxury lemon curd
a little sifted icing sugar

1 Preheat the oven to 190°C/Fan 170°C/Gas 5. Grease two 20cm (8 in) round sandwich tins and line the bases with non-stick baking paper.

2 Put the eggs and sugar in a large heatproof bowl over a pan of lightly simmering water and whisk until the mixture is thick, white and creamy and leaves a thick trail when the whisk is lifted from the mixture. Remove from the heat and whisk for a further 2 minutes.

3 Sift in the flour and very carefully fold it in with a metal spoon.

4 Divide the mixture between the tins, level out evenly and bake in the preheated oven for 20 minutes, or until well risen and the tops of the sponges spring back when lightly pressed with a finger.

5 Turn out on to a wire rack, remove the paper and leave to cool.

6 To make the filling, whisk the cream until thick then fold in the lemon curd.

7 Sandwich the cakes together with the lemon cream and dust the top with icing sugar before serving.

# HONEY AND ALMOND CAKE

*The sort of special cake that is just right for when Granny comes to tea.
As this basic cake mixture is not rich, it is best to make the base on the
day or day before it is needed.*

**SERVES 6**

150g (5 oz) baking
   spread, from fridge
100g (4 oz) light
   muscovado sugar
2 tbsp runny honey
3 large eggs
150g (5 oz) self-raising
   flour
50g (2 oz) ground
   almonds
2 tbsp milk
1 tsp almond extract

**For the filling and
   topping**
100g (4 oz) butter,
   softened
2 tbsp runny honey
½ tsp almond extract
150g (5 oz) icing sugar,
   sifted
50g (2 oz) flaked
   almonds, toasted

1 Preheat the oven to 160°C/Fan 140°C/Gas 3. Grease a 17.5cm
(7 in) deep cake tin and line the base with non-stick baking paper.

2 Measure all the ingredients for the cake into a large mixing bowl
and beat with an electric mixer until well blended and smooth.

3 Turn the mixture into the tin, level the top and bake in the
preheated oven for about 45–55 minutes, or until well risen
and the tops of the cakes spring back when lightly pressed
with a finger.

4 Leave to cool in the tin for about 10 minutes then turn out,
remove the paper and finish cooling on a wire rack.

5 To make the filling and topping, measure the butter, honey,
almond extract and icing sugar into a bowl and mix well until
thoroughly blended.

6 Slice the cake in half horizontally and sandwich together
with half of the icing. Coat the sides of the cake with half of
the remaining icing and roll in the toasted almonds so that the
sides are evenly coated. Use the remaining icing to cover the
top of the cake then sprinkle with the remaining almonds.

# CLASSIC GENOESE

*Best filled with whipped cream and soft fruit.*

**SERVES 6**

3 large eggs
90g (3½ oz) caster sugar
90g (3½ oz) self-raising
   flour
40g (1½ oz) butter,
   melted and cooled

*For the filling*
150ml (¼ pint) double
   cream
about 100g (4 oz)
   raspberries or sliced
   strawberries
about 1 level tbsp
   caster sugar

**1** Preheat the oven to 180°C/Fan 160°C/Gas 4. Grease two 17.5cm (7 in) round sandwich tins and line the bases with non-stick baking paper.

**2** Put the eggs and sugar in a heatproof bowl over a pan of hot water and whisk until the mixture is thick, white and creamy and leaves a trail when the whisk is lifted out of the bowl. Remove from the heat and whisk for a further 2 minutes.

**3** Sift the flour and carefully fold it into the mixture with a metal spoon.

**4** Drizzle the butter around the edge of the mixture and carefully fold it in until it is evenly blended.

**5** Divide the mixture between the tins, level out evenly and bake in the preheated oven for 20–25 minutes, or until golden brown, well risen and the tops of the sponges spring back when lightly pressed with a finger.

**6** Turn out and leave to cool on a wire rack.

**7** To make the filling, whisk the cream until it is thick and the mixture forms peaks. Fold in the fruit and sugar to taste.

**8** When the cakes are cold, sandwich them together with the cream and fruit mixture.

# SPICY GINGER CAKE

*This is a good basic ginger cake that will keep very well in an airtight tin; in fact, it is better to keep it for three or four days before cutting.*

**MAKES 16 SQUARES**

100g (4 oz) baking
   spread, from fridge
175g (6 oz) golden syrup
50g (2 oz) black treacle
50g (2 oz) dark soft
   brown sugar
150ml (¼ pint) milk
2 large eggs
225g (8 oz) plain flour
2 level tsp ground
   mixed spice
1 level tsp bicarbonate
   of soda
2 level tsp ground
   ginger

1 Preheat the oven to 160°C/Fan 140°C/Gas 3. Grease a 20cm (8 in) square cake tin and line with non-stick baking paper.

2 Measure the spread, syrup, treacle and sugar into a small saucepan and heat gently until the spread has melted.

3 Remove from the heat, add the milk and leave on one side to cool.

4 Beat the eggs then stir them into the cooled mixture.

5 Sift the flour into a bowl, together with the spice, bicarbonate of soda and ginger. Make a well in the centre and stir in the cooled milk and treacle mixture until well blended and smooth.

6 Pour into the tin and bake in the preheated oven for about 1¼ hours, or until risen and golden brown.

7 Turn out and leave to cool on a wire rack.

8 Cut into 16 squares and store in an airtight tin until required.

# SWISS ROLL

*Home-made Swiss roll is not difficult if you follow these instructions and if you weigh all the ingredients accurately.*

**SERVES 8**

4 large eggs, at room temperature
100g (4 oz) caster sugar, warmed
100g (4 oz) self-raising flour

*For the filling*
caster sugar, to sprinkle
about 5 tbsp raspberry jam

**1** Preheat the oven to 220°C/Fan 200°C/Gas 7. Grease a Swiss roll tin 33 x 23cm (13 x 9 in) and line with non-stick baking paper.

**2** Whisk the eggs and sugar together in a large bowl until the mixture is light and creamy and the whisk leaves a trail when lifted out.

**3** Sift the flour into the mixture and carefully fold it in with a metal spoon.

**4** Turn the mixture into the tin and give it a gentle shake so the mixture finds its own level, making sure that it spreads evenly into the corners. Bake in the preheated oven for about 10 minutes, or until the sponge is golden brown and begins to shrink from the edges of the tin.

**5** While the cake is cooking, cut a piece of non-stick baking paper a little bigger than the tin and sprinkle it with caster sugar.

**6** Remove the cake from the oven and invert on to the sugared paper. Quickly loosen the paper from the bottom of the cake and peel it off. To make rolling easier, make a score mark 2.5cm (1 in) in from one of the short edges, being careful not to cut through. Fold the narrow strip created by the score mark down and begin rolling, using the paper to keep a firm roll. Leave for a few minutes with the paper still around it so it will settle. Lift on to a wire rack.

**7** When cool, remove the paper and spread the cake with jam, taking it almost to the edges. Reroll and sprinkle with more sugar before serving.

# SUPERB CARROT CAKE

*This is a wonderfully gooey version. You could decorate it with walnut halves, if liked. I've added a small bake variation – these are easier for packed lunches, quicker to bake but equally delicious.*

**SERVES 12**

225g (8 oz) self-raising flour
1 level tsp baking powder
150g (5 oz) light muscovado sugar
50g (2 oz) walnuts, chopped
100g (4 oz) carrots, washed, trimmed and coarsely grated
2 ripe bananas, mashed
2 large eggs
150ml (¼ pint) sunflower oil

**For the topping**

50g (2 oz) butter, softened
50g (2 oz) full-fat cream cheese
150g (5 oz) icing sugar, sifted
½ tsp vanilla extract

1 Preheat the oven to 180°C/Fan 160°C/Gas 4. Grease a 20cm (8 in) deep cake tin and line the base with non-stick baking paper.

2 Sift together the flour and baking powder into a large bowl and stir in the sugar. Add the nuts, carrots and bananas and mix lightly.

3 Make a well in the centre, add the eggs and oil and beat until well blended.

4 Turn the mixture into the tin and bake in the preheated oven for about 1¼ hours, or until golden brown and shrinking slightly from the sides of the tin. A skewer inserted into the centre of the cake should come out clean.

5 Turn out, remove the paper and leave to cool on a wire rack.

6 To make the topping, place all the ingredients in a bowl and beat with an electric mixer until well blended and smooth. Spread over the cake and rough up with a fork. Leave in a cool place to harden slightly before serving.

**VARIATION: MINI CARROT CAKES**
Prepare the cake mix as above and use to fill 12 muffin cases set in a muffin tin. Cook for 25–30 minutes until well risen and lightly brown. Prepare the topping as above and, once the cakes have cooled, use to top each cake.

# BATTENBURG CAKE

*This may not be as 'fast' as some of the other cakes in the book, but it is such a family favourite that we felt it was important to include it. If you have a special 17.5cm (7 in) Battenburg tin with divisions then do use it but I've included here instructions on how to make your own divisions in a square tin.*

**SERVES 8**

100g (4 oz) baking spread, from fridge
100g (4 oz) caster sugar
2 large eggs
100g (4 oz) self-raising flour
½ level tsp baking powder
50g (2 oz) ground almonds
1 tsp vanilla extract
3 tsp milk
a few drops red colouring
225g (8 oz) marzipan

**For the icing**

100g (4 oz) icing sugar, plus extra to dust
40g (1½ oz) butter, softened
1 tsp vanilla extract
a few drops milk, if needed

1 Preheat the oven to 160°C/Fan 140°C/Gas 3. Grease a 17.5cm (7 in) square cake tin. Cut out a piece of parchment-lined foil or baking paper that is 7.5 cm (3 in) longer than one side of the tin. Fold the paper in half widthways with the foil-side on the inside. Open out the paper and push up the centre fold to make a 4cm (1½ in) pleat. Line the base of the tin with this, foil side down, making any adjustments to ensure the pleat runs down the centre of the tin.

2 Measure the baking spread, sugar, eggs, flour, baking powder and ground almonds into a large bowl and beat with a wooden spoon for about 2–3 minutes until smooth, slightly lighter in colour and glossy looking.

3 Spoon just very slightly more than half the mixture into a separate bowl and stir in the vanilla extract and 1½ teaspoons of the milk. Set aside.

4 Mix the red colouring with the remaining 1½ teaspoons of milk, then stir this into the other bowl of mixture.

5 Spoon the vanilla mixture into one half of the tin and the pink mixture into the other half. Level the surface of each half with a knife. Check the paper divider is still straight and in the middle.

6 Bake in the centre of the preheated oven for about 35–40 minutes, or until well risen and shrinking slightly from the sides of the tin.

RECIPE CONTINUED OVERLEAF

7 Leave to cool in the tin for a few minutes then turn out, remove the paper and finish cooling on a wire rack.

8 To make the icing, sift the icing sugar into a medium bowl and measure in the butter and the vanilla extract. Beat everything together with a wooden spoon until soft and smooth. Add a few drops of milk if the icing is a bit stiff.

9 Trim the crispy outer edges off the cooled cake with a serrated knife, then cut and trim, if necessary, into 4 equal lengthways strips – you need 2 vanilla and 2 pink strips. Lay 1 vanilla and 1 pink strip side by side, then use a little of the butter icing to stick them together. Spread a bit more icing on top. Stick the remaining 2 strips together with icing and lay these on top of the bottom cakes so when the 4 are put together they create a chequerboard effect. Cut two pieces of string, one that is the length of the assembled cake and one that will wrap all around it, in order to help you roll the marzipan to the correct size. Finally, spread a bit more icing over the top of the assembled chequerboard.

10 Lightly dust a work surface with sifted icing sugar and roll out the marzipan into an oblong the length of the cake and sufficiently wide to wrap around the cake, using the pieces of string as your measuring guide. Lay the iced side of the cake on to the marzipan, positioning it so when you lift up one long side, it perfectly covers one side of the cake (this way the join will be neatly in the corner). Spread the rest of the icing over the remaining 3 sides of the cake (not the ends). Brush off any crumbs from the marzipan and work surface so they don't stick. Roll the cake over in the marzipan, pressing to neatly cover it, then brush the corner join lightly with water, pressing it to seal. (Try to avoid touching the marzipan with wet fingers as it will mark.) Turn the cake over so the join is on the bottom. Trim a slim slice from each end of the cake to neaten and show off the chequerboard effect. Smooth the marzipan with your hands so their warmth will give it a smooth finish.

# SHOO FLY PIE

*This rather sweet pie comes from the Deep South of the USA and is a great favourite. Serve it cut into wedges when you are looking for something different to offer at your coffee morning. The pastry must be thin in order for it to cook without blind baking.*

**SERVES 8**

*For the shortcrust pastry*
175g (6 oz) plain flour
1 level tbsp icing sugar
75g (3 oz) butter, cubed
1 large egg, beaten
about 1 tbsp cold water

*For the filling*
100g (4 oz) seedless
   raisins
50g (2 oz) light or dark
   muscovado sugar
3 tbsp hot water
¼ level tsp bicarbonate
   of soda

*For the topping*
100g (4 oz) plain flour
½ level tsp ground
   cinnamon
¼ level tsp ground
   ginger
¼ level tsp ground
   nutmeg
50g (2 oz) unsalted
   butter
50g (2 oz) light or dark
   muscovado sugar

1 You will need a 20cm (8 in) loose-bottomed, deep, fluted tart tin.

2 To make the pastry, measure the flour, icing sugar and butter into a food processor. Whizz until breadcrumb stage. Add the egg and water and whizz again until a dough is formed. Roll out thinly on a floured work surface and use to line the tin. Prick the base and sides all over with a fork and leave to chill in the fridge for 30 minutes.

3 Preheat the oven to 190°C/Fan 170°C/Gas 5 and put a heavy baking sheet in the oven on the shelf just above the centre.

4 To make the topping, sift the flour and spices together into a bowl and rub in the butter until the mixture resembles fine breadcrumbs. Carefully stir in the sugar.

5 Remove the pastry from the fridge and cover with the raisins. Mix the sugar with the hot water and bicarbonate of soda and pour over the raisins.

6 Sprinkle the topping over the raisins then place on the baking sheet in the preheated oven and bake for about 25–30 minutes, or until golden brown.

7 Leave to cool in the tin then lift out on to a serving plate. Serve cut into wedges.

# MINCEMEAT AND ALMOND TART

*Serve either warm or cold. A rather different way of serving this traditional tart, the mincemeat complements the almond flavour well.*

**SERVES 8**

**For the shortcrust pastry**
175g (6 oz) plain flour
1 level tbsp icing sugar
75g (3 oz) butter, cubed
1 large egg
about 1 tbsp cold water

**For the filling**
100g (4 oz) butter
100g (4 oz) caster sugar
2 large eggs, beaten
100g (4 oz) ground
     almonds
1 tsp almond extract
4 good tbsp mincemeat

1 You will need a 20cm (8 in) loose-bottomed, deep, fluted tart tin.

2 To make the pastry, measure the flour, icing sugar and butter into a food processor. Whizz until breadcrumb stage. Add the egg and water and whizz again, until a dough is formed. Roll out thinly on a floured work surface. Line the tin and prick the base and sides. Leave to chill in the fridge for 30 minutes.

3 Preheat the oven to 200°C/Fan 180°C/Gas 6.

4 To make the filling, heat the butter in a small pan until it has just melted. Stir in the sugar, beaten egg, ground almonds and almond extract.

5 Spread the mincemeat over the base of the pastry case, then spread the buttery filling on top. Bake in the preheated oven for about 30 minutes, or until golden brown and the filling springs back when lightly pressed with a finger.

6 Leave to cool on a wire rack then lift out on to a serving plate. Serve cut into wedges.

# ALMOND BAKEWELL TART

*This makes a delicious tart and, if you like, you could make the mixture as small individual tarts but this will, of course, take longer. The pastry must be thin in order for it to cook without blind baking.*

**SERVES 8**

*For the shortcrust pastry*
175g (6 oz) plain flour
1 level tbsp icing sugar
75g (3 oz) butter, cubed
1 large egg, beaten
about 1 tbsp cold water

*For the filling*
100g (4 oz) butter, softened
100g (4 oz) caster sugar
2 large eggs
100g (4 oz) ground almonds
1 tsp almond extract
4 good tbsp raspberry jam
a few flaked almonds

**1** You will need a 20cm (8 in) loose-bottomed, deep, fluted tart tin.

**2** To make the pastry, measure the flour, icing sugar and butter into a food processor. Whizz until breadcrumb stage. Add the egg and water and whizz again until a dough is formed. Roll out thinly on a floured work surface. Line the tin and prick the base and sides. Leave to chill in the fridge for 30 minutes.

**3** Preheat the oven to 200°C/Fan 180°C/Gas 6 and put a baking sheet in the oven on the shelf just above the centre.

**4** To make the filling, measure the butter and sugar into a food processor and whizz until light and fluffy. Add the eggs and whizz again. Finally, add the ground almonds and extract and whizz one last time.

**5** Spread the base of the flan with the jam then pour the filling over the top. Sprinkle with the flaked almonds and place the tin on the hot baking sheet. Bake in the preheated oven for about 30–35 minutes, or until the pastry is pale golden brown at the edges and the filling is set.

**6** Remove from the oven and leave to cool in the tin. Serve cut into wedges.

# SUMMER RASPBERRY SHORTBREAD

*This looks very good when served for a special coffee morning. Make sure that everyone has a small fork and serve the shortbread with a dollop of thick cream.*

**SERVES 8**

125g (4½ oz) plain flour
75g (3 oz) butter
40g (1½ oz) caster sugar
350g (12 oz) raspberries
3 tbsp redcurrant jelly
double cream, whipped,
 to serve

**1** Sift the flour into a bowl. Add the butter and sugar and rub in the butter until the mixture resembles fine breadcrumbs. Knead together, then turn on to a table and knead lightly for 3 minutes until the mixture is smooth.

**2** Roll or pat out the shortbread on a baking sheet to a round 5mm (¼ in) thick and 20cm (8 in) in diameter. Crimp the edges and leave to chill in the fridge for 30 minutes.

**3** Preheat the oven to 160°C/Fan 140°C/Gas 3.

**4** Bake in the preheated oven for about 25–30 minutes, or until a pale golden brown at the edges.

**5** Leave on the baking sheet until quite cold, then lift off and place on a serving dish.

**6** Arrange the raspberries all over the shortbread.

**7** Heat the redcurrant jelly in a small pan until it is dissolved and smooth and then brush it over the fruit and leave to set.

**8** Serve the shortbread in wedges with a blob of thick cream.

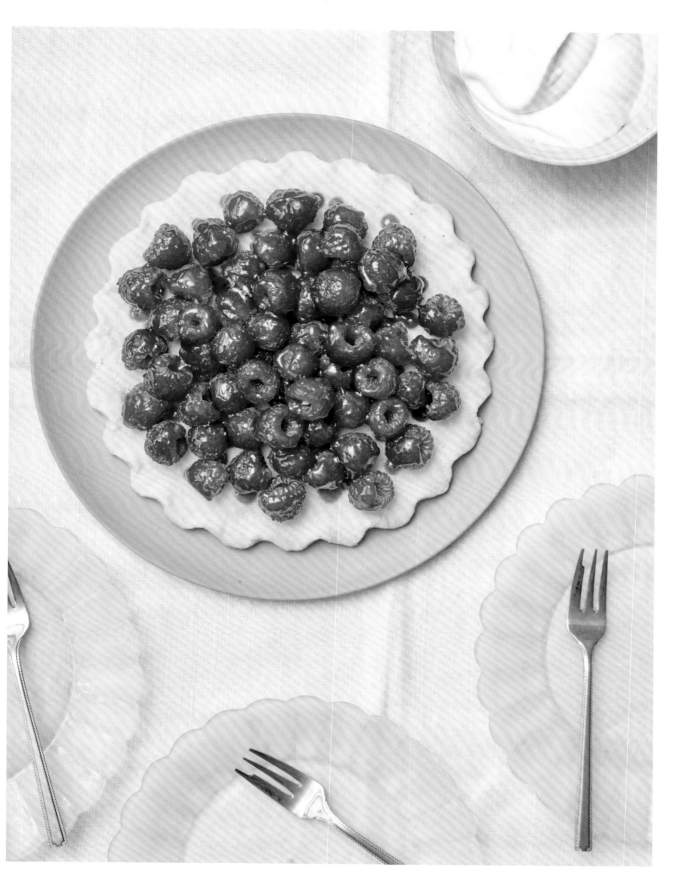

# TRADITIONAL TREACLE TART

*Treacle tart is one of those favourites that is so easy to prepare and always has the family coming back for second helpings. I try to keep breadcrumbs in the freezer so that they are easily at hand for recipes such as this. There will be a little pastry left over so use it for a few jam tarts.*

**SERVES 8**

**For the shortcrust pastry**
175g (6 oz) plain flour
1 level tbsp icing sugar
75g (3 oz) butter, cubed
1 large egg, beaten
about 1 tbsp cold water

**For the filling**
about 9 good tbsp
    golden syrup
about 150g (5 oz) fresh
    white or brown
    breadcrumbs
finely grated zest and
    juice of 1 large lemon

1 You will need a 20cm (8 in) loose-bottomed, fluted tart tin.

2 To make the pastry, measure the flour, icing sugar and butter into a food processor. Whizz until breadcrumb stage. Add the egg and water and whizz again until a dough is formed. Roll out thinly on a floured work surface. Line the tin and prick the base and sides. Leave to chill in the fridge for 30 minutes.

3 Preheat the oven to 200°C/Fan 180°C/Gas 6.

4 Heat the syrup in a large pan over a medium heat until runny and then stir in the breadcrumbs, lemon zest and juice. (It may be necessary to add a few more breadcrumbs if the mixture looks too runny.)

5 Turn the mixture into the pastry case, level out the top and bake in the preheated oven for 10 minutes. Reduce the oven temperature to 180°C/Fan 160°C/Gas 4 and bake for a further 20–25 minutes, or until the tart is cooked.

6 Leave to cool in the tin then lift out on to a serving plate. Serve cut into wedges.

# ORANGE CHEESECAKE

*A lovely no-bake cheesecake.*

**SERVES 8**

300ml smooth fresh orange juice from a carton

1 x 135g packet orange jelly, cubed

350g (12 oz) full-fat cream cheese, at room temperature

25g (1 oz) caster sugar

150ml (¼ pint) double cream, whipped

1 x 298g can mandarin segments

*For the base*

150g (5 oz) digestive biscuits, crushed

25g (1 oz) demerara sugar

50g (2 oz) butter, melted

1 You will need a 20cm (8 in) loose-bottomed springform cake tin.

2 Measure the orange juice into a saucepan and place over a medium heat until hand hot. Remove from the heat and add the cubes of jelly. Stir until dissolved.

3 Pour into a bowl and leave to chill in the fridge until the jelly has thickened and is starting to set.

4 Meanwhile, make the base by mixing together the biscuits, sugar and melted butter. Spread over the base of the cake tin and place in the fridge to set.

5 Measure the cream cheese into a large bowl and whisk with the caster sugar. Add the almost-set jelly and then fold in the whipped cream. Mix until smooth. Turn into the tin on top of the crumb base and return to the fridge for about 4 hours, until set.

6 When ready to serve, remove the cheesecake from the tin and place it on a serving dish. Drain the mandarins and arrange around the top of the cheesecake.

# VANILLA BAKED CHEESECAKE

*A rich and moist cheesecake.*

**SERVES 8**

75g (3 oz) butter
8–10 digestive biscuits, crushed (about 125g/4½ oz)
2 x 280g tubs full-fat cream cheese
50g (2 oz) plain flour
2 tsp vanilla extract
2 large eggs
100g (4 oz) caster sugar
150ml (¼ pint) double cream
150ml (¼ pint) sour cream
1 level tbsp icing sugar, sifted
1 ripe mango, peeled and finely sliced
1 large passion fruit

1 Preheat the oven to 180°C/Fan 160°C/Gas 4. Lightly grease the base of a 20cm (8 in) loose-bottomed cake or springform tin and line with non-stick baking paper.

2 Melt the butter in a pan over a gentle heat. Remove from the heat and measure in the biscuits. Mix together very well.

3 Turn into the tin and press flat over the base using a spoon.

4 Measure the cream cheese and flour into another bowl and beat using an electric hand-held whisk until smooth. Add the vanilla, eggs, sugar and double cream and whisk again until well blended.

5 Pour over the crumb base and bake in the preheated oven for about 30 minutes, or until well risen and just set around the edges.

6 Remove from the oven and rest for 10 minutes to allow the top of the cheesecake to become level and flat.

7 Return to the oven for a final 10 minutes, until the cheesecake is just set with a slight wobble in the middle.

8 Loosen the edges then leave to cool in the tin. When cold, remove from the tin and leave to chill in the fridge.

9 Mix the sour cream and icing sugar together in a small bowl and then spread over the cold cheesecake. Arrange the mango and seeds and pulp of the passion fruit over the top of the cheesecake before serving.

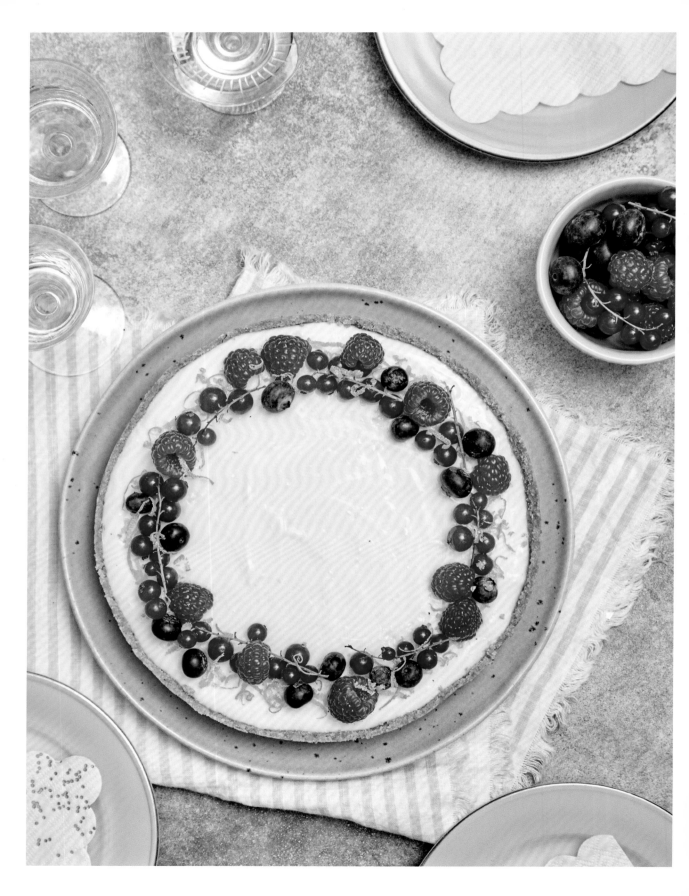

# THOMAS'S FLAN

*This flan is named after my elder son and was one of his favourites to make growing up. Serve it with any fruit that is to hand; blueberries are nice or, if it is summer, use strawberries or raspberries. In winter, canned mandarin oranges look very good.*

**SERVES 6–8**

*For the flan case*
75g butter
8–10 digestive biscuits, crushed (about 125g/4½ oz)

*For the filling and decoration*
1 x 397g can full-fat condensed milk
150ml (¼ pint) double cream
zest and juice of 2 lemons
a selection of fresh fruits, to decorate

1 Line the base and sides of a 20cm (8 in) loose-bottomed cake or springform tin.

2 Melt the butter in a pan over a gentle heat. Remove from the heat and measure in the biscuits. Mix together very well.

3 Turn into the tin and press flat over the base and sides of the tin using a spoon. Leave to chill in the fridge.

4 Meanwhile, to make the topping, measure the condensed milk, cream and lemon juice into a bowl and beat with an electric hand-held whisk until well blended. Pour into the flan case and level the top.

5 Leave to chill in the fridge for at least 4 hours, until set.

6 When ready to serve, lift out of the tin and decorate with the finely grated lemon zest and fruits of your choice.

# COCONUT AND JAM CAKE

*Delicious served warm as a pudding.*

**SERVES 6**
50g (2 oz) butter,
  softened
175g (6 oz) caster sugar
4 large eggs
100g (4 oz) self-raising
  flour
500ml (18 fl oz) milk
75g (3 oz) desiccated
  coconut
4 tbsp raspberry jam
double cream, to serve

**1** Preheat the oven to 180°C/Fan 160°C/Gas 4 and lightly grease a 25cm (10 in) shallow ovenproof dish.

**2** Measure the butter, sugar and eggs into a bowl and beat using an electric hand-held whisk until smooth. Add the flour and whisk again. While whisking, pour the milk in a steady stream to make a smooth batter. Fold in the coconut.

**3** Spread a thin layer of jam over the base of the dish and then pour in the batter from a low height.

**4** Bake in the preheated oven for about 45–50 minutes, or until well risen and golden brown with a slight wobble in the middle.

**5** Serve warm with cream.

# RASPBERRY CREAM PAVLOVA

*This is really not difficult and does not take too long to make. It needs just an hour, undisturbed, in the oven. You must then turn off the heat and forget it until it is quite cold; do not open the oven door and peep.*

**SERVES 8**
3 large egg whites
175g (6 oz) caster sugar
1 tsp white wine
    vinegar
1 level tsp cornflour
225g (8 oz) fresh
    raspberries
300ml (½ pint) double
    cream, whipped
icing sugar, to decorate

**1** Preheat the oven to 160°C/Fan 140°C/Gas 3 and lay a sheet of silicone paper or non-stick baking paper on a baking sheet and mark a 20cm (8 in) circle on it.

**2** Place the egg whites in a large bowl and whisk on high speed with an electric whisk until they form soft peaks.

**3** Add the sugar, a generous dessertspoonful at a time, whisking on maximum speed until all the sugar has been added and the meringue is stiff and shiny.

**4** Blend the vinegar with the cornflour in a little bowl until smooth and whisk it into the meringue mixture.

**5** Spread the meringue out to cover the circle on the baking sheet – building up the sides so that they are higher than the centre. Place in the middle of the preheated oven and immediately turn down the heat to 150°C/Fan 130°C/Gas 2. Bake for about 1 hour, or until the pavlova is a pale creamy colour. Turn the oven off and leave in the oven for 1 hour to become cold.

**6** Remove from the oven, lift off the paper and place on a serving dish.

**7** Keep some of the raspberries back for decoration and put the rest in a large bowl with the cream and lightly fold together.

**8** Pile the cream and raspberry mixture into the centre of the pavlova and leave to stand for 1 hour in a cool place or fridge before serving. Just before serving decorate with the reserved raspberries and dredge with a little icing sugar.

# TRAYBAKES AND FAMILY CAKES

# BASIC TRAYBAKE

*The basic recipe is economical and made with large families, coffee mornings and bazaars in mind.*

**MAKES 16 PIECES**

225g (8 oz) baking
    spread, from fridge
225g (8 oz) caster sugar
275g (10 oz) self-raising
    flour
1 level tsp baking
    powder
4 large eggs
4 tbsp milk

*To finish*
a little sifted icing sugar
    (optional)

**1** Preheat the oven to 180°C/Fan 160°C/Gas 4. Grease a 30 x 23cm (12 x 9 in) traybake tin and line with non-stick baking paper.

**2** Measure all the ingredients into a large bowl and beat with an electric mixer until light and fluffy.

**3** Turn the mixture into the tin and level the top. Bake in the preheated oven for 30–35 minutes, or until the cake has shrunk a little from the sides of the tin and springs back when pressed in the centre with your fingertips.

**4** Leave to cool in the tin.

**5** Sprinkle with icing sugar, if liked, and cut into 16 pieces.

---

**VARIATION: VANILLA TRAYBAKE**
Add 1 teaspoon of vanilla extract to the traybake ingredients and continue to prepare as above.

# FRUIT TRAYBAKE

*Adding some dried fruit to the basic traybake recipe gives a lovely and easy alternative. Use whatever you have in the cupboard, though currants work particularly well.*

**MAKES 16 PIECES**
225g (8 oz) baking spread, from fridge
225g (8 oz) caster sugar
275g (10 oz) self-raising flour
1 level tsp baking powder
4 large eggs
4 tbsp milk
200g (7 oz) sultanas
100g (4 oz) ready-to-eat dried apricots, finely chopped
1 level tbsp demerara sugar

**1** Preheat the oven to 180°C/Fan 160°C/Gas 4. Grease a 30 x 23cm (12 x 9 in) traybake tin and line with non-stick baking paper.

**2** Measure all the ingredients except the dried fruit and demerara sugar into a large bowl and beat with an electric mixer until well blended. Stir in the sultanas and apricots.

**3** Turn the mixture into the tin and level the top. Bake in the preheated oven for 30–35 minutes, or until the cake has shrunk a little from the sides of the tin and springs back when pressed in the centre with your fingertips. Halfway through the baking time, remove the cake from the oven and sprinkle the top with the demerara sugar.

**4** Leave to cool in the tin.

**5** Cut into 16 pieces to serve.

# VANILLA AND CHOCOLATE MARBLE TRAYBAKE

*This is a lovely variation on the basic traybake – a visual treat perfect for the school cake sale.*

**MAKES 16 PIECES**

225g (8 oz) baking
    spread, from fridge
225g (8 oz) caster sugar
275g (10 oz) self-raising
    flour
1 level tsp baking
    powder
4 large eggs
4 tbsp milk
1 tsp vanilla extract
25g (1 oz) cocoa powder

*To finish*
a little sifted icing
    sugar (optional)

1 Preheat the oven to 180°C/Fan 160°C/Gas 4. Grease a 30 x 23cm (12 x 9 in) traybake tin and line with non-stick baking paper.

2 Measure all the ingredients except the cocoa into a large bowl and beat well with an electric mixer until light and fluffy. Place half the mixture in another bowl and add the cocoa powder. Mix until well blended.

3 Place large spoonfuls of both cake mixtures in the tin, then swirl the two colours together using a skewer to create a marbled effect.

4 Bake in the preheated oven for 30–35 minutes, or until the cake has shrunk a little from the sides of the tin and springs back when pressed in the centre with your fingertips.

5 Leave to cool in the tin.

6 Sprinkle with icing sugar, if liked, and cut into 16 pieces.

# LEMON DRIZZLE TRAYBAKE

*It's important to spoon the glaze on the cake while it's still warm so the lemon juice soaks in properly.*

**MAKES 16 PIECES**

225g (8 oz) baking spread, from fridge
225g (8 oz) caster sugar
275g (10 oz) self-raising flour
1 level tsp baking powder
4 large eggs
4 tbsp milk
finely grated zest of 2 lemons

*For the glaze*
juice of 2 lemons
175g (6 oz) granulated sugar

1 Preheat the oven to 180°C/Fan 160°/Gas 4. Grease a 30 x 23cm (12 x 9 in) traybake tin and line with non-stick baking paper.

2 Measure all the ingredients into a large bowl and beat with an electric mixer until well blended.

3 Turn the mixture into the tin and level the top. Bake in the preheated oven for about 35–40 minutes, or until the cake has shrunk a little from the sides of the tin and springs back when pressed in the centre with your fingertips.

4 While the cake is baking, make the glaze. Mix the lemon juice and sugar together in a bowl and stir to a runny consistency.

5 As soon as the traybake comes out of the oven, pour the lemon and sugar glaze over the surface of the warm cake, spreading to cover and leave to set.

6 Once cold, cut into 16 pieces.

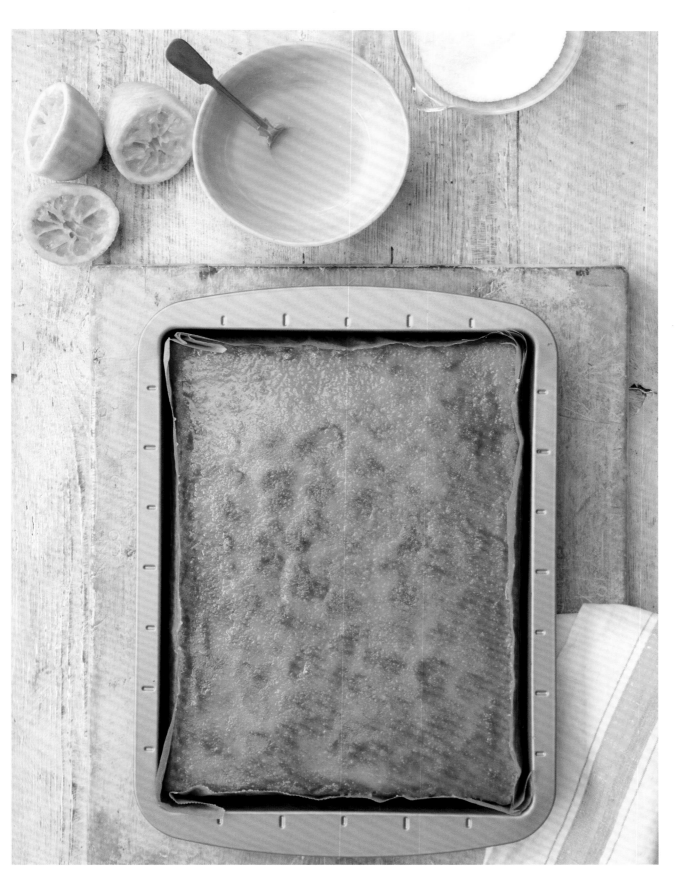

# SPICED TREACLE TRAYBAKE

*When the cake is cooked and cold it looks nice if sprinkled with sifted icing sugar.*

**MAKES 16 PIECES**

225g (8 oz) baking
   spread, from fridge
115g (4¼ oz) caster
   sugar
275g (10 oz) self-raising
   flour
1 level tsp baking
   powder
4 large eggs
4 tbsp milk
200g (7 oz) black treacle
1½ level tsp ground
   mixed spice

**To finish**
a little sifted icing sugar
   (optional)

1 Preheat the oven to 180°C/Fan 160°C/Gas 4. Grease a 30 x 23cm (12 x 9 in) traybake tin and line with non-stick baking paper.

2 Measure all the ingredients into a large bowl and beat with an electric mixer until well blended.

3 Turn the mixture into the tin and level the top. Bake in the preheated oven for about 35–40 minutes, or until the cake has shrunk a little from the sides of the tin and springs back when pressed in the centre with your fingertips.

4 Leave to cool in the tin.

5 Sprinkle with icing sugar, if liked, and cut into 16 pieces.

# ICED CHERRY TRAYBAKE

*Ring the changes by using fresh cherries in season.*

**MAKES 16 PIECES**

225g (8 oz) baking
   spread, from fridge
225g (8 oz) caster sugar
275g (10 oz) self-raising
   flour
1 level tsp baking
   powder
4 large eggs
4 tbsp milk

*For the icing*

75g (3 oz) butter,
   softened
225g (8 oz) icing sugar,
   sifted
1–2 tbsp milk
1 tsp vanilla extract

*To finish*

16 natural glacé
   cherries, halved

1 Preheat the oven to 180°C/Fan 160°C/Gas 4. Grease a 30 x 23cm (12 x 9 in) traybake tin and line with non-stick baking paper.

2 Measure all the cake ingredients into a large bowl and beat with an electric mixer until well blended.

3 Turn the mixture into the tin and level the top. Bake in the preheated oven for about 30 minutes, or until the cake has shrunk a little from the sides of the tin and springs back when pressed in the centre with your fingertips.

4 Leave to cool in the tin.

5 Measure the icing ingredients into a bowl and beat with an electric mixer until well blended. Spread over the top of the cake, mark into 16 and decorate each piece with 2 glacé cherry halves.

# LEMON AND LIME TRAYBAKE

*This is a lovely and citrusy traybake.*

**MAKES 16 PIECES**

225g (8 oz) baking
    spread, from fridge
225g (8 oz) caster sugar
275g (10 oz) self-raising
    flour
4 large eggs
1 level tsp baking
    powder
2 level tbsp lemon curd
finely grated zest of
    1 large lemon
finely grated zest of
    1 large lime

**For the icing**

300g (10½ oz) icing
    sugar, sifted
3–4 tbsp lemon and
    lime juice

1 Preheat the oven to 180°C/Fan 160°C/Gas 4. Grease a 30 x 23cm (12 x 9 in) traybake tin and line with non-stick baking paper.

2 Measure the baking spread, caster sugar, flour, eggs, baking powder, lemon curd and half of the lemon and lime zests into a mixing bowl. Beat together using an electric mixer until light and fluffy.

3 Turn the mixture into the tin and level the top. Bake in the preheated oven for about 30–35 minutes, or until well risen and the top of the sponge springs back when lightly pressed with a finger.

4 Leave to cool in the tin.

5 To make the icing, measure the icing sugar and lemon and lime juices into a bowl. Whisk until smooth, then spread over the cake.

6 Sprinkle with the remaining lemon and lime zest before cutting into 16 pieces.

# POPPY SEED AND LEMON TRAYBAKE

*Full of zesty lemon flavour.*

**MAKES 16 PIECES**
225g (8 oz) baking
   spread, from fridge
225g (8 oz) caster sugar
275g (10 oz) self-raising
   flour
1 level tsp baking
   powder
4 large eggs
4 tbsp milk
finely grated zest
   of 2 lemons
2 level tbsp poppy seeds

**For the glaze**
juice of 2 lemons
200g (7 oz) granulated
   sugar

1 Preheat the oven to 180°C/Fan 160°C/Gas 4. Grease a 30 x 23cm (12 x 9 in) traybake tin and line with non-stick baking paper.

2 Measure all the ingredients except the poppy seeds into a large bowl and beat with an electric mixer until light and fluffy. Fold in the poppy seeds, turn the mixture into the tin and level the top.

3 Bake in the preheated oven for 30–35 minutes, or until the cake has shrunk a little from the sides of the tin and springs back when pressed in the centre with your fingertips.

4 While the cake is baking, make the glaze. Mix the lemon juice and sugar together in a bowl and stir to a runny consistency.

5 As soon as the traybake comes out of the oven, pour the lemon glaze over the surface of the warm cake, spreading to cover, and leave to set.

6 Once cold, cut into 16 pieces.

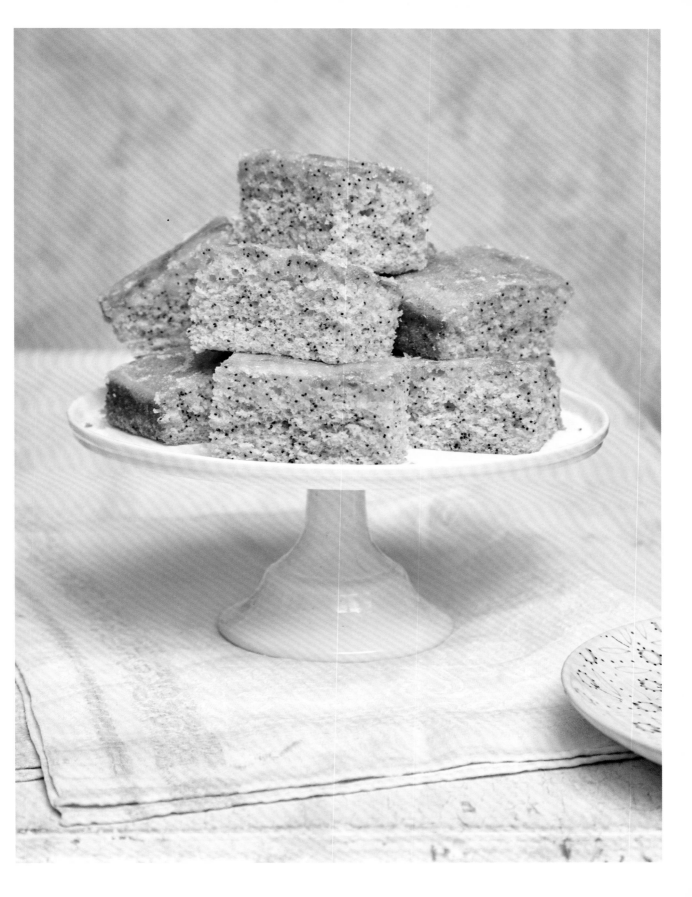

# COCONUT AND FRUIT TRAYBAKE

*Ideal to include in a lunch box or to take on a picnic.*

**MAKES 16 PIECES**

225g (8 oz) baking spread, from fridge
225g (8 oz) self-raising flour
2 level tsp ground mixed spice
150g (5 oz) desiccated coconut
225g (8 oz) light muscovado sugar
4 large eggs
2 tbsp milk
200g (7 oz) sultanas
100g (4 oz) seedless raisins
icing sugar, to dust

**1** Preheat the oven to 180°C/Fan 160°C/Gas 4. Grease a 30 x 23cm (12 x 9 in) traybake tin and line with non-stick baking paper.

**2** Place all the ingredients except the dried fruit and icing sugar in a bowl and beat with an electric mixer until light and fluffy. Stir in the sultanas and raisins.

**3** Turn the mixture into the tin and level the top. Bake in the preheated oven for about 40–45 minutes, or until golden brown and springing back when lightly pressed with your fingertips.

**4** Leave to cool in the tin.

**5** Dust with icing sugar and cut into 16 pieces.

# COFFEE FUDGE TRAYBAKE

*This traybake has a very mild coffee flavour which, strangely enough, is popular with children.*

**MAKES 20 PIECES**
175g (6 oz) baking
    spread, from fridge
175g (6 oz) caster sugar
3 large eggs
1 tbsp coffee essence
175g (6 oz) self-raising
    flour
¾ level tsp baking
    powder

*For the icing*
75g (3 oz) butter,
    softened
225g (8 oz) icing sugar,
    sifted
1 tbsp milk
1 tbsp coffee essence

**1** Preheat the oven to 160°C/Fan 140°C/Gas 3. Grease a 30 x 23cm (12 x 9 in) traybake tin and line with non-stick baking paper.

**2** Measure the traybake ingredients into a bowl and beat well with an electric mixer until well blended.

**3** Turn the mixture into the tin and level the top. Bake in the preheated oven for 40 minutes, or until the cake is well risen and shrinking away from the sides of the tin. The cake will spring back when lightly pressed with your fingertips.

**4** Leave to cool in the tin.

**5** To make the icing, put the butter, icing sugar, milk and coffee essence in a bowl and beat until smooth. Spread over the cake and cut into 20 pieces.

# CONFETTI TRAYBAKE

*This looks so pretty – it's a simple, fast cake for school fêtes or coffee mornings.*

**MAKES 20 PIECES**

225g (8 oz) baking spread, from fridge
225g (8 oz) caster sugar
275g (10 oz) self-raising flour
1 level tsp baking powder
4 large eggs
4 tbsp milk
1 tsp vanilla extract

**To finish**

300g (10½ oz) icing sugar
3 tbsp boiling water
2 level tbsp hundreds and thousands

1 Preheat the oven to 180°C/Fan 160°C/Gas 4. Grease a 30 x 23cm (12 x 9 in) traybake tin and line with non-stick baking paper.

2 Measure all the traybake ingredients into a large bowl and beat with an electric mixer until light and fluffy.

3 Turn the mixture into the tin and level the top. Bake in the preheated oven for 30–35 minutes, or until the cake has shrunk a little from the sides of the tin and springs back when pressed in the centre with your fingertips.

4 Leave to cool in the tin.

5 Mix the icing sugar and water together in a bowl to make a smooth paste. Spread over the cold cake and sprinkle with hundreds and thousands. Cut into 20 pieces.

# BLUEBERRY AND VANILLA TRAYBAKE

*A modern classic combination of flavours.*

**MAKES 16 PIECES**

225g (8 oz) baking spread, from fridge
225g (8 oz) caster sugar
275g (10 oz) self-raising flour
1 level tsp baking powder
4 large eggs
4 tbsp milk
1 tsp vanilla extract

*For the icing*

50g (2 oz) butter, softened
100g (4 oz) icing sugar
1 tsp vanilla extract
250g (9 oz) full-fat mascarpone cheese

*To finish*

225g (8 oz) blueberries

1 Preheat the oven to 180°C/Fan 160°C/Gas 4. Grease a 30 x 23cm (12 x 9 in) traybake tin and line with non-stick baking paper.

2 Measure all the traybake ingredients into a large bowl and beat with an electric mixer until light and fluffy.

3 Turn the mixture into the tin and level the top. Bake in the preheated oven for 30–35 minutes, or until the cake has shrunk a little from the sides of the tin and springs back when pressed in the centre with your fingertips.

4 Leave to cool in the tin.

5 To make the icing, whisk the butter and icing sugar together in a bowl. Add the vanilla and mascarpone and whisk again until smooth. Spread over the top of the traybake, decorate with the blueberries and cut into 16 pieces.

# COFFEE AND WALNUT TRAYBAKE

*A traybake version of the family favourite.*

**MAKES 16 PIECES**

2 level tbsp instant coffee granules
2 tbsp boiling water
225g (8 oz) baking spread, from fridge
225g (8 oz) caster sugar
275g (10 oz) self-raising flour
1 level tsp baking powder
4 large eggs
4 tbsp milk

*To finish*

1 level tbsp instant coffee granules
1 tbsp boiling water
100g (4 oz) butter, softened
175g (6 oz) icing sugar
1 tbsp milk
50g (2 oz) walnuts, chopped

**1** Preheat the oven to 180°C/Fan 160°C/Gas 4. Grease a 30 x 23cm (12 x 9 in) traybake tin and line with non-stick baking paper.

**2** Measure the coffee and boiling water into a large mixing bowl. Stir until dissolved. Leave to cool for 2–3 minutes.

**3** Add the remaining cake ingredients to the bowl and beat with an electric mixer until light and fluffy.

**4** Turn the mixture into the tin and level the top. Bake in the preheated oven for 30–35 minutes, or until the cake has shrunk a little from the sides of the tin and springs back when pressed in the centre with your fingertips.

**5** Leave to cool in the tin.

**6** To make the icing, measure the coffee and boiling water into a mixing bowl. Stir until dissolved. Leave to cool for 2–3 minutes. Add all of the remaining ingredients except the walnuts to the bowl and beat using an electric mixer until pale and creamy, then spread over the cake.

**7** Sprinkle with the walnuts and cut into 16 pieces to serve.

# GINGER TRAYBAKE WITH COFFEE ICING

*Lovely and moist, this cake keeps well in an airtight tin. The brown sugar and treacle give the cake a slightly denser sponge, rather than it being light.*

**MAKES 18 PIECES**

150g (4 oz) baking spread, from fridge
75g (3 oz) black treacle
75g (3 oz) golden syrup
75g (3 oz) light muscovado sugar
3 level tsp ground ginger
300g (10½ oz) self-raising flour
100ml (3½ fl oz) milk
3 large eggs

*For the icing*

225g (8 oz) icing sugar, sifted
2 tsp coffee essence
about 2½ tbsp water

1 Preheat the oven to 160°C/Fan 140°C/Gas 3. Grease a 30 x 23cm (12 x 9 in) traybake tin and line with non-stick baking paper.

2 Measure the spread, black treacle, golden syrup and sugar into a pan and heat gently until the spread has melted.

3 Measure the ginger and flour into a bowl and pour over the melted mixture. Add the milk and eggs and beat with an electric mixer until thoroughly blended. Pour into the tin.

4 Bake in the preheated oven for about 1 hour, or until well risen and the top springs back when lightly pressed with your fingertips.

5 Leave to cool in the tin for a few moments then turn out, remove the paper and finish cooling on a wire rack.

6 To make the icing, measure the icing sugar into a bowl, add the coffee essence and sufficient water to give a smooth icing. Spread evenly over the top of the cake and leave to set.

7 Cut into 18 pieces to serve.

# SPICED TOFFEE TRAYBAKE

*A lovely traybake for a coffee morning or cake sale.*

**MAKES 16 PIECES**

225g (8 oz) baking spread, from fridge
225g (8 oz) light muscovado sugar
275g (10 oz) self-raising flour
1 level tsp baking powder
4 large eggs
2 tbsp milk
2 tbsp treacle
1 level tsp ground ginger
½ level tsp ground mixed spice
1 level tsp ground cinnamon

*For the icing*

100g (4 oz) butter, softened
175g (6 oz) icing sugar
25g (1 oz) light muscovado sugar
1 tsp vanilla extract
1 tbsp milk
1 level tsp ground cinnamon

**1** Preheat the oven to 180°C/Fan 160°C/Gas 4. Grease a 30 x 23cm (12 x 9 in) traybake tin and line with non-stick baking paper.

**2** Measure all the traybake ingredients into a large bowl and beat with an electric mixer until light and fluffy.

**3** Turn the mixture into the tin and level the top. Bake in the preheated oven for 30–35 minutes, or until the cake has shrunk a little from the sides of the tin and springs back when pressed in the centre with your fingertips.

**4** Leave to cool in the tin.

**5** To make the icing, measure all of the ingredients into a large bowl and beat with an electric mixer until pale and creamy. Spread over the cold cake and cut into 16 pieces to serve.

# RED VELVET BROWNIE TRAYBAKE

*This has a heavier texture to the other traybakes in this chapter, which makes it more like a brownie. It is delicious and was one of the favourite bakes when we were photographing the recipes for the book!*

**MAKES 18 PIECES**

300g (10½ oz) Bournville chocolate, broken into pieces
200g (7 oz) butter
200g (7 oz) caster sugar
4 large eggs
1 tsp vanilla extract
150g (5 oz) self-raising flour
15g (½ oz) red gel colouring

*For the icing*

50g (2 oz) butter, softened
50g (2 oz) full-fat cream cheese
150g (5 oz) icing sugar
½ tsp vanilla extract

**1** Preheat the oven to 180°C/Fan 160°C/Gas 4. Grease a 30 x 23cm (12 x 9 in) traybake tin and line with non-stick baking paper.

**2** Measure the chocolate and butter into a heatproof bowl. Melt over a pan of simmering water until smooth and runny.

**3** Remove the bowl from the heat and add the sugar, eggs, vanilla and flour. Beat with an electric mixer until well blended and smooth. Stir in the red gel.

**4** Turn the mixture into the tin and level the top. Bake in the preheated oven for 35–40 minutes, or until risen and a crust has formed on the surface. The middle should feel just firm when pressed with your fingertips.

**5** Leave to cool in the tin. The brownie may dip slightly in the centre.

**6** To make the icing, measure all the ingredients into a large bowl and beat using an electric mixer until pale and creamy. Spread over the brownie and swirl the top.

**7** Cut into 18 pieces to serve.

# ROYAL GINGER SQUARES

*If you have had a jar of stem ginger on the shelf for a while this is a good way of putting it to use. The squares are topped with a simple ginger icing.*

**MAKES 20 SQUARES**

175g (6 oz) baking spread, from fridge
175g (6 oz) light muscovado sugar
175g (6 oz) self-raising flour
¾ level tsp baking powder
1½ level tsp ground ginger
3 large eggs
40g (1½ oz) stem ginger, very finely chopped

*For the topping*
175g (6 oz) icing sugar, sifted
3–4 tbsp ginger syrup from the jar

1 Preheat the oven to 180°C/Fan 160°C/Gas 4. Grease a 30 x 23cm (12 x 9 in) traybake tin and line with non-stick baking paper.

2 Measure the spread, sugar, flour, baking powder, ginger and eggs into a large bowl and beat with an electric mixer until well blended.

3 Turn the mixture into the tin, level the top and bake in the preheated oven for about 20 minutes. Sprinkle over the finely chopped ginger and continue cooking for a further 15 minutes, or until the sponge is golden brown and springs back when pressed in the centre with your fingertips.

4 Leave to cool in the tin then turn out, remove the paper and finish cooling on a wire rack.

5 To make the icing, blend the icing sugar with the ginger syrup until smooth – loosen with a few drops of water, if necessary. Drizzle or spoon over the cake and leave to set.

6 Cut into 20 squares to serve.

# BUTTERSCOTCH CAKE

*A simple sponge with a very tasty icing on top. It is ideal for cutting into squares or pieces to serve at a coffee morning.*

**MAKES 24 PIECES**

225g (8 oz) baking spread, from fridge
225g (8 oz) light muscovado sugar
4 large eggs
225g (8 oz) self-raising flour
1 level tsp baking powder

*For the icing*

100g (4 oz) butter, softened
175g (6 oz) icing sugar
1 tsp vanilla extract
25g (1 oz) light muscovado sugar
2 tbsp milk

1 Preheat the oven to 180°C/Fan 160°C/Gas 4. Grease a 30 x 23cm (12 x 9 in) traybake tin and line with non-stick baking paper.

2 Measure all the traybake ingredients into a bowl and beat with an electric mixer until light and fluffy.

3 Turn the mixture into the tin, level the top and bake in the preheated oven for about 30 minutes, or until well risen and golden brown. The cake will have shrunk slightly from the sides of the tin.

4 Leave to cool in the tin.

5 To make the icing, measure all of the ingredients into a bowl and whisk together until light and creamy. Spread over the surface of the cake.

6 Cut into 24 pieces to serve.

# CRUNCHY HAZELNUT PIECES

*The crunchy topping sinks slightly into the cake during baking and gives a lovely flavour to a simple sponge mixture.*

**MAKES 18 PIECES**

175g (6 oz) baking spread, from fridge
175g (6 oz) caster sugar
3 large eggs
225g (8 oz) self-raising flour

*For the topping*

50g (2 oz) butter
175g (6 oz) demerara sugar
2 level tsp ground cinnamon
3 level tbsp plain flour
50g (2 oz) roasted hazelnuts, chopped

1 Preheat the oven to 180°C/Fan 160°C/Gas 4. Grease a 30 x 23cm (12 x 9 in) traybake tin and line with non-stick baking paper.

2 To make the topping, melt the butter in a small saucepan then remove the pan from the heat and add all the remaining ingredients. Leave to cool.

3 Measure all the traybake ingredients into a bowl and beat with an electric mixer until light and fluffy.

4 Turn the mixture into the tin, level the top and sprinkle with the topping. Bake in the preheated oven for about 35–40 minutes, or until the mixture is well risen and has shrunk from the sides of the tin.

5 Leave to cool in the tin.

6 Cut into 18 pieces to serve.

# HONEY CAKE

*A simple tasty cake that is made all in one saucepan – nice and easy on the washing up!*

**MAKES 16 PIECES**

150g (5 oz) baking spread, from fridge
100g (4 oz) dark or light muscovado sugar
150ml (¼ pint) clear honey
1 tbsp milk
2 large eggs
200g (7 oz) self-raising flour
a few flaked almonds

1 Preheat the oven to 180°C/Fan 160°C/Gas 4. Grease a 30 x 23cm (12 x 9 in) traybake tin and line with non-stick baking paper.

2 Put the spread, sugar, honey and milk in a saucepan and heat gently until the spread has melted and the sugar has dissolved. Leave on one side to cool.

3 Beat the eggs into the honey mixture one at a time then stir in the flour.

4 Pour the mixture into the tin and sprinkle the top with almonds. Bake in the preheated oven for 30–35 minutes, or until well risen and the cake has shrunk back from the sides of the tin.

5 Turn out, remove the paper, then leave to cool on a wire rack.

6 Cut into 16 pieces and store in an airtight tin.

CHAPTER THREE

# CHOCOLATE
# BAKES

# CLASSIC CHOCOLATE SPONGE SANDWICH

*A classic chocolate sponge – such an easy and quick cake.*

**SERVES 8**

2 good tbsp cocoa
     powder
4 tbsp hot water
225g (8 oz) baking
     spread, from fridge
225g (8 oz) caster sugar,
     plus extra to sprinkle
4 large eggs
225g (8 oz) self-raising
     flour
1 level tsp baking
     powder
Bournville chocolate,
     grated or curled,
     to decorate

*For the icing*
75g (3 oz) butter,
     softened
225g (8 oz) icing sugar,
     sifted

1 Preheat the oven to 180°C/Fan 160°C/Gas 4. Grease two 20cm (8 in) round sandwich tins and line the bases with non-stick baking paper.

2 Blend the cocoa with the water in a small bowl and leave to cool.

3 Measure the spread, sugar, eggs, flour and baking powder into a large mixing bowl, add the cooled cocoa liquid and beat with an electric mixer until thoroughly blended.

4 Divide the mixture between the tins, level out evenly and bake in the preheated oven for about 25–30 minutes, or until well risen and the tops of the sponges spring back when lightly pressed with your fingertips.

5 Leave to cool in the tins for a few minutes then turn out, remove the paper and finish cooling on a wire rack.

6 To make the icing, blend the butter with the icing sugar and use half to sandwich the cakes together when they are completely cold. Use the other half to ice the top.

7 Lift on to a serving plate and decorate with curls or gratings of chocolate.

# CAN'T-GO-WRONG CHOCOLATE CAKE

*A moist chocolate cake that really can't go wrong and keeps well.*

**SERVES 8**

190g (6½ oz) plain flour
2 level tbsp cocoa
    powder
1 level tsp bicarbonate
    of soda
1 level tsp baking
    powder
150g (5 oz) caster sugar
2 tbsp golden syrup
2 large eggs
150ml (¼ pint)
    sunflower oil
150ml (¼ pint) milk

*For the icing*
50g (2 oz) butter
4 level tbsp cocoa
    powder, sifted
3 tbsp milk
150g (5 oz) icing sugar,
    sifted

1 Preheat the oven to 160°C/Fan 140°C/Gas 3. Grease two 20cm (8 in) round sandwich tins and line the bases with non-stick baking paper.

2 Sift the dry ingredients into a large bowl and then make a well in the centre. Add the syrup, eggs, oil and milk. Beat well with an electric mixer until thoroughly blended.

3 Pour the mixture into the tins and bake in the preheated oven for 30–35 minutes, or until the cake springs back when lightly pressed with your fingertips.

4 Turn out on to a wire rack, remove the paper and leave to cool.

5 To make the icing, melt the butter in a small pan over a gentle heat. Add the cocoa, stir to blend and cook gently for 1 minute. Stir in the milk and icing sugar, remove from the heat and mix very well. Leave on one side, stirring occasionally, until the icing thickens.

6 Sandwich the cakes with half the icing and then use the remainder to ice the top, swirling with a knife to give an attractive appearance.

# SIMPLE CHOCOLATE CAKE WITH FUDGE ICING

*A fabulous chocolate cake. This delicious cake can be made in a 20cm (8 in) foil container, allowed to cool in the container, and then iced. This makes it perfect to take on a picnic or to sell at a cake sale.*

**SERVES 8**

2 level tbsp cocoa powder
2 tbsp hot water
100g (4 oz) baking spread, from fridge
100g (4 oz) caster sugar
2 large eggs
100g (4 oz) self-raising flour
1 level tsp baking powder

*For the icing*

25g (1 oz) cocoa powder, sifted
40g (1½ oz) butter, softened
2–3 tbsp milk
100g (4 oz) icing sugar, sifted

**1** Preheat the oven to 180°C/ Fan 160°C/Gas 4. Grease a 20cm (8 in) deep cake tin and line with non-stick baking paper. If using a foil container, grease this well.

**2** Blend the cocoa with the hot water in a large bowl and leave to cool. Add the remaining cake ingredients to the bowl and beat with an electric mixer until light and fluffy.

**3** Spoon into the tin and bake in the preheated oven for 20–25 minutes, or until the cake has shrunk slightly from the sides of the tin and springs back when lightly pressed with a finger.

**4** Turn out, remove the paper and leave to cool on a wire rack.

**5** To make the icing, measure the cocoa, butter, milk and icing sugar into a bowl. Beat well to a light, smooth consistency.

**6** Spread over the top of the cake and swirl attractively with a round-bladed knife. Leave to set before serving.

# MELT-IN-THE-MOUTH CHOCOLATE DESSERT CAKE

*This is a heavenly, light chocolate cake to serve with a fork. The cake itself contains no flour and has a good chocolate flavour. Do expect it to sink slightly on cooling.*

**SERVES 8**

6 large eggs
150g (5 oz) caster sugar
50g (2 oz) cocoa powder, sifted

**For the filling and topping**

300ml (½ pint) double cream, whipped
25g (1 oz) icing sugar, sifted (optional)
wafer-thin mint chocolates, to decorate (optional)

1 Preheat the oven to 180°C/Fan 160°C/Gas 4. Grease two 20cm (8 in) round sandwich tins and line the bases with non-stick baking paper.

2 Separate the eggs by putting the whites in a large bowl and the yolks in a smaller bowl. Add the caster sugar to the yolks and beat with an electric mixer until thick.

3 Whisk the egg whites in a separate bowl with an electric whisk until the mixture forms stiff peaks. Add 2 tablespoons of the whisked whites to the yolk mixture, mix thoroughly, then add this to the whites and gently fold in until thoroughly blended. Finally fold in the cocoa powder.

4 Divide the mixture between the tins, level out evenly and bake in the preheated oven for about 25 minutes, or until just beginning to shrink back from the sides of the tins. They will rise but will drop back down towards the end of the baking.

5 Leave to cool in the tins for about 5 minutes then turn out, remove the paper and finish cooling on a wire rack.

6 Sweeten the cream with the icing sugar, if using, then sandwich the cakes together with half the cream and spread the remainder on top.

7 Break the mint thins in half, if using, and arrange around the top of the cake before serving.

# AMERICAN CHOCOLATE CAKE

*A really large, moist chocolate cake that is quick to make.*

**SERVES 8**

275g (10 oz) self-raising flour
3 level tbsp cocoa powder
175g (6 oz) caster sugar
1 level tsp bicarbonate of soda
300ml (½ pint) milk
150ml (¼ pint) sunflower oil
3 tbsp golden syrup
½ tsp vanilla extract

*For the icing*
25g (1 oz) cocoa powder, sifted
25g (1 oz) butter, softened
200g (7 oz) icing sugar, sifted
2–3 tbsp milk

1 Preheat the oven to 180°C/Fan 160°C/Gas 4. Grease two 20cm (8 in) round sandwich tins and line the bases with non-stick baking paper.

2 Sift the flour, cocoa and sugar into a bowl and make a well in the centre.

3 Dissolve the bicarbonate of soda in 1 tablespoon of the milk and then pour this into the flour with the remaining milk, oil, syrup and vanilla extract and beat with an electric mixer to make a smooth batter.

4 Pour the mixture into the tins and bake in the preheated oven for about 40 minutes, or until the cakes spring back when lightly pressed with a fingertip.

5 Turn out on to a wire rack and leave to cool.

6 To make the icing, place the cocoa, butter and icing sugar in a bowl and beat together until smooth, adding the milk to loosen. Use to sandwich the cakes together.

# MILK CHOCOLATE CAKE

*A richer chocolate cake. Use a small can of evaporated milk; this will give you enough for both the cake and the icing.*

**SERVES 8**

200g (7 oz) self-raising flour
225g (8 oz) caster sugar
25g (1 oz) cocoa powder, sifted
100g (4 oz) baking spread, from fridge
2 large eggs
150ml (¼ pint) evaporated milk

*For the icing*
25g (1 oz) baking spread
25g (1 oz) cocoa powder, sifted
2 tbsp evaporated milk
125g (4½ oz) icing sugar, sifted
Bournville chocolate, grated into shards, to decorate (optional)

*For the filling*
150ml (½ pint) double cream, lightly whipped

**1** Preheat the oven to 180°C/Fan 160°C/Gas 4. Grease two 20cm (8 in) round sandwich tins and line the bases with non-stick baking paper.

**2** Place all the cake ingredients together in a bowl and beat with an electric mixer until light and fluffy.

**3** Divide the mixture between the two tins, level out evenly and bake in the preheated oven for 25–30 minutes, or until the cakes are well risen and have shrunk slightly from the sides of the tin. They should spring back when lightly pressed with the fingertips.

**4** Turn out and leave to cool on a wire rack.

**5** To make the icing, put the spread and cocoa in a saucepan and heat gently until the spread has melted, stirring continuously. Remove from the heat and beat in the evaporated milk and icing sugar until the mixture is thick.

**6** Sandwich the cakes together with the whipped cream, then spread the icing over the top of the cake. Sprinkle with chocolate shards, if liked, and leave to set. The icing will lose its shine over time.

# MOCHA GÂTEAU

*This cake is always very popular with young and old alike.*

**SERVES 8**

175g (6 oz) self-raising flour

175g (6 oz) caster sugar

175g (6 oz) baking spread, from fridge

3 large eggs

1 tbsp coffee essence

¾ level tsp baking powder

*For the icing*

100g (4 oz) butter, softened

225g (8 oz) icing sugar, sifted

1½ tbsp coffee essence

40g (1½ oz) drinking chocolate

Bournville chocolate shavings, to decorate

1 Preheat the oven to 180°C/Fan 160°C/Gas 4. Grease two 20cm (8 in) round sandwich tins and line the bases with non-stick baking paper.

2 Measure the cake ingredients into a large bowl and beat with an electric mixer until well blended.

3 Divide the mixture between the tins, level out evenly and bake in the preheated oven for about 35 minutes, or until the cakes are well risen and have shrunk slightly away from the sides of the tins.

4 Turn out, remove the paper and leave to cool on a wire rack.

5 To make the icing, measure the butter, icing sugar, coffee essence and drinking chocolate into a bowl and beat until smooth and well blended. Use half to sandwich the cakes together and the remainder to cover the top. Mark the cake attractively with a fork or round-bladed knife and then decorate with chocolate shavings.

# CHOCOLATE BUTTON CAKE

*A fabulous chocolate cake which is quick to make. Store in the fridge.*

**SERVES 8**

2 level tbsp cocoa
    powder
2 tbsp hot water
175g (6 oz) baking
    spread, from fridge
175g (6 oz) caster sugar
3 large eggs
175g (6 oz) self-raising
    flour
1 level tsp baking
    powder
a few drops peppermint
    extract

**For the filling and
topping**

300ml (½ pint) double
    cream, whipped
1 x 119g packet giant
    chocolate buttons,
    to decorate

1 Preheat the oven to 180°C/Fan 160°C/Gas 4. Grease two 20cm (8 in) round sandwich tins and line the bases with non-stick baking paper.

2 Measure the cocoa and water into the bottom of a large mixing bowl and mix to a smooth paste. Add the remaining ingredients and beat well with an electric mixer until well blended.

3 Divide the mixture between the tins, level out evenly and bake in the preheated oven for about 20–25 minutes, or until well risen and springing back when lightly pressed with a finger.

4 Leave to cool in the tins for about 5 minutes then turn out, remove the paper and finish cooling on a wire rack.

5 Sandwich the cakes together with half the whipped cream and spread the remaining cream on top. Decorate with chocolate buttons.

# CHOCOLATE ORANGE CAKE

*This lovely moist cake is made in one bowl.*

**SERVES 6–8**
125g (4½ oz) self-raising flour
15g (½ oz) cocoa powder
½ level tsp baking powder
100g (4 oz) baking spread, from fridge
75g (3 oz) caster sugar
1 tbsp golden syrup
2 large eggs
50g (2 oz) Bournville chocolate, grated
finely grated zest and juice of 1 orange

**1** Preheat the oven to 160°C/Fan 140°C/Gas 3. Grease a 17.5cm (7 in) round cake tin and line with non-stick baking paper.

**2** Measure all the ingredients into a large mixing bowl and beat with an electric mixer until well blended.

**3** Turn the mixture into the tin, level the top and bake in the preheated oven for about 45 minutes, or until well risen, has shrunk slightly from the sides of the tin and the top springs back when lightly pressed with your fingertips.

**4** Turn out and leave to cool on a wire rack.

# DEVIL'S FOOD CAKE

*This is my version of the traditional American recipe; the yoghurt gives
a lovely texture.*

**SERVES 8**

225g (8 oz) caster sugar
50g (2 oz) cocoa powder, sifted
1 x 150g tub natural yoghurt
100g (4 oz) baking spread, from fridge
4 large eggs
225g (8 oz) self-raising flour
1 level tsp baking powder

**For the filling and topping**

75g (3 oz) butter, softened
175g (6 oz) icing sugar, sifted
75g (3 oz) Bournville chocolate, melted and cooled
apricot jam

1 Preheat the oven to 190°C/Fan 170°C/Gas 5. Grease two 20cm (8 in) round sandwich tins and line the bases with non-stick baking paper.

2 Measure all the ingredients for the cake into a large mixing bowl and beat with an electric mixer until well blended and smooth.

3 Divide the mixture between the tins, level out evenly and bake in the preheated oven for about 25–30 minutes, or until well risen, shrinking away from the sides of the tins and the tops spring back when lightly pressed with your fingertips.

4 Leave to cool in the tins for a few minutes then turn out, remove the paper and finish cooling on a wire rack.

5 To make the icing, cream the butter with the icing sugar until light and fluffy then stir in the melted chocolate.

6 Sandwich the sponges together with a layer of apricot jam and half the icing. Spread the remaining icing on top. Decorate the cake by drawing squiggly lines in the icing with a fork.

# CHOCOLATE CUPCAKES

*These are delicious topped with a fresh raspberry but would look lovely with a nasturtium flower, too.*

**MAKES 12**
150g (5 oz) baking spread, from fridge
150g (5 oz) caster sugar
115g (4¼ oz) self-raising flour
35g (1¼ oz) cocoa powder
3 large eggs
1 level tsp baking powder
a handful of fresh raspberries, to decorate (optional)

**For the icing**
100g (4 oz) Bournville chocolate, broken into pieces
4 tbsp water
25g (1 oz) butter
175g (6 oz) icing sugar, sifted

**1** Preheat the oven to 200°C/Fan 180°C/Gas 6 and arrange 12 muffin cases in a muffin tin.

**2** Measure all the ingredients for the cakes except the raspberries into a large mixing bowl and beat with an electric mixer until well blended and smooth.

**3** Divide the mixture between the paper cases and bake in the preheated oven for about 20 minutes, or until the cakes are well risen and spring back when lightly pressed with a finger.

**4** Remove from the oven and leave to cool on a wire rack.

**5** For the icing, measure the chocolate, water and butter into a heatproof bowl and heat gently over a pan of simmering water until the chocolate and butter have melted. Remove from the heat, beat until smooth then stir in the icing sugar until thoroughly mixed.

**6** Leave to cool until just beginning to set, then spread a little on the top of each cake. If liked, top each cake with a raspberry, or other fruit in season, before serving.

# NO-BAKE CHOCOLATE JULIETTE

*This chocolate loaf is very rich, so serve it in thin slices – and offer pastry forks to your guests.*

**SERVES 8–10**

200g (7 oz) butter
225g (8 oz) Bournville chocolate, broken into pieces
2 tbsp rum or brandy
175g (6 oz) Nice biscuits

1 Line a small 450g (1 lb) loaf tin with cling film.

2 Measure the butter and chocolate into a heatproof bowl. Place the bowl on top of a pan of boiling water and heat gently until the mixture has melted and is smooth and runny. Stir in the rum or brandy.

3 Break the biscuits into 1.25cm (½ in) pieces and stir into the chocolate mixture.

4 Pack the chocolate mixture into the tin and smooth the top with the back of a spoon.

5 Leave to chill in the fridge for about 6 hours, until set.

6 Turn out on to a serving plate and peel off the cling film. Cut into 8–10 slices to serve.

# MOCHA BRANDY GÂTEAU

*You will enjoy both making and eating this. If you have a deep loaf tin, rather than a long, shallow one, you may need a few more sponge fingers to line it.*

**SERVES 6–8**

4 tbsp brandy
1 level tbsp instant coffee granules
6 tbsp boiling water
10 sponge fingers, each one halved widthways
cocoa powder, to dust (optional)
Bournville chocolate shavings, to decorate (optional)

***For the filling***

50g (2 oz) caster sugar
6 tbsp water
100g (4 oz) Bournville chocolate, chopped into small pieces
2 large egg yolks, beaten
300ml (½ pint) double cream

1 Wet the inside of a 900g (2 lb) loaf tin and line with cling film.

2 Measure the brandy, coffee and boiling water into a heatproof bowl. Mix well, then quickly dip the sponge fingers into the liquid. Line the sides and edges of the tin with the sponges.

3 To make the filling, measure the sugar and water into a saucepan and dissolve the sugar slowly over a low heat. Increase the heat and bring to the boil. Boil for a few seconds until you have a thin syrup.

4 Remove from the heat and add the chocolate. Stir until completely melted.

5 Add the egg yolks and mix well.

6 Lightly whip the double cream in a large bowl. Fold in the chocolate mixture and mix until smooth.

7 Pour into the tin and level the top. Cover with cling film and leave to chill in the fridge for about 6 hours, or until set.

8 Remove the cling film from the top of the loaf tin, turn upside down on to a serving plate and remove the tin and remaining cling film. Dust with cocoa powder and decorate with chocolate shavings, if liked.

9 Cut into 6–8 slices to serve.

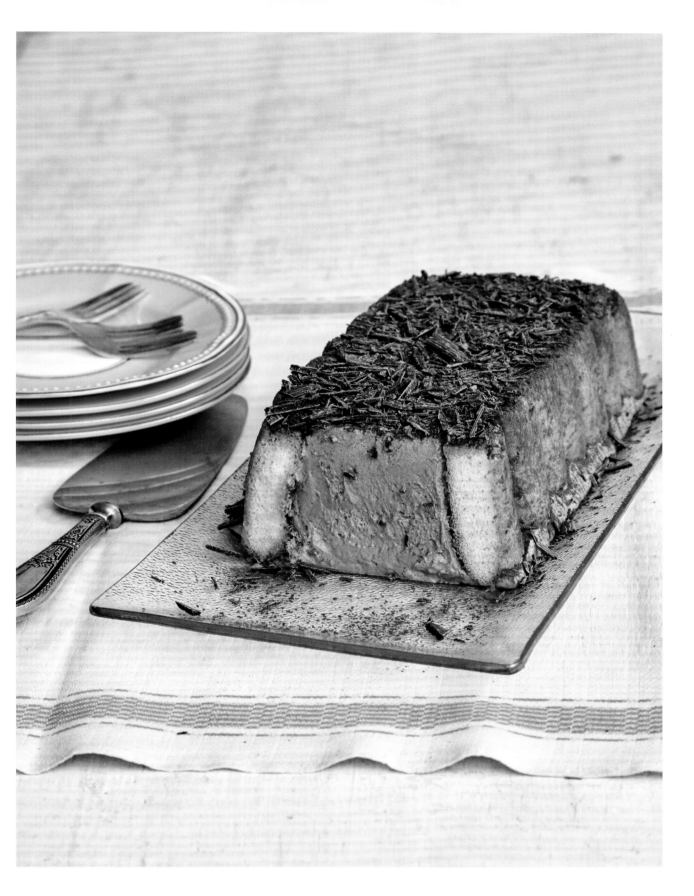

# MILLIONAIRE'S SHORTBREAD

*These are not ultra-quick to make but are great favourites with all ages. Do not expect the caramel to harden – it doesn't. The shortbread is gooey and sticky to eat.*

**MAKES 21**

**For the base**
100g (4 oz) butter, softened
50g (2 oz) caster sugar
150g (5 oz) plain flour

**For the caramel**
100g (4 oz) butter
75g (3 oz) caster sugar
2 tbsp golden syrup
½ x 397g can condensed milk

**For the topping**
100g (4 oz) Bournville chocolate, broken into pieces

1 Preheat the oven to 180°C/Fan 160°C/Gas 4 and grease a 27.5 x 17.5cm (11 x 7 in) baking tin.

2 Place all the ingredients for the base in a bowl and beat to a firm dough. (The mixture may require a light kneading with the hand to come together.)

3 Press into the tin with the back of a spoon. Prick with a fork then bake in the preheated oven for 25–30 minutes, until a pale brown.

4 While the shortbread is baking, prepare the caramel. Measure all the ingredients into a saucepan and heat gently until melted. Bring the mixture to the boil and leave to bubble for 10–15 minutes until it is caramel coloured. Stir continuously, preferably with a flat-based wooden spoon that can get into the sides of the pan and prevent the mixture from catching.

5 Remove from the heat and leave to cool slightly.

6 When the shortbread is cooked and has cooled for about 5 minutes, pour the caramel over the top and leave on one side.

7 Break the chocolate into pieces and place in a small heatproof bowl standing over a saucepan of water. Heat gently until the chocolate has melted and is smooth.

8 Pour the chocolate in a steady stream over the caramel to make a thin layer of chocolate on top. Before the chocolate has hardened, drag a fork gently through it to make swirling patterns. Leave to set.

9 Cut into 21 pieces to serve.

# CHOCOLATE ÉCLAIRS

*Everybody's favourite. Be sure to dry out the pastry cases thoroughly after baking before filling with cream, so that they are crisp to eat. Ideally, the éclairs should be filled just before serving so that they retain this crispiness.*

**MAKES 20**
50g (2 oz) butter
150ml (¼ pint) water
65g (2½ oz) strong
    plain flour
2 large eggs, beaten

**For the filling**
300ml (½ pint) double
    cream, whipped

**For the icing**
225g (8 oz) icing sugar
1 level tbsp cocoa
    powder
1 tbsp rum
1–2 tbsp warm water

**1** Preheat the oven to 200°C/Fan 180°C/Gas 6 and grease two large baking sheets.

**2** Put the butter and water in a saucepan and bring to the boil, stirring occasionally. Remove from the heat and add the flour all at once and beat until the mixture forms a ball. Leave to cool slightly then gradually beat in the eggs to make a smooth, shiny paste.

**3** Place the mixture in a piping bag fitted with a 1.25cm (½ in) plain pipe. Pipe 20 éclairs, each about 5cm (2 in) long, on to the baking sheets, leaving room for them to expand during cooking. Bake in the preheated oven for about 20 minutes, or until well risen and golden brown.

**4** Remove from the oven and split one side of each éclair so that the steam can escape. Leave to cool on a wire rack. If the insides of the split éclairs are still moist, then return them to the oven to dry out for a further 5 minutes.

**5** Pipe or spoon the whipped cream into the middle of the base of the éclairs and replace the top.

**6** To make the icing, sift the icing sugar and cocoa into a bowl and stir in the rum and just sufficient warm water to make a thick icing. Spear each éclair with a fork and dip the tops in the icing. Leave to set and then serve on the day they are made and filled.

# COFFEE AND CHOCOLATE ÉCLAIRS

*These are one of my most favourite things to eat. The coffee filling makes them that little bit more special.*

**MAKES 20**
50g (2 oz) butter
150ml (¼ pint) water
65g (2½ oz) strong
   plain flour
2 large eggs, beaten

*For the filling*
50g (2 oz) icing sugar,
   sifted
1 tbsp coffee essence
300ml (½ pint) double
   cream, whipped

*For the icing*
50g (2 oz) Bournville
   chocolate, broken
   into pieces
2 tbsp water
1 level tbsp butter
75g (3 oz) icing sugar,
   sifted

1 Preheat the oven to 200°C/Fan 180°C/Gas 6 and grease two large baking sheets.

2 Put the butter and water in a saucepan and bring to the boil, stirring occasionally. Remove from the heat and add the flour all at once and beat until the mixture forms a ball. Leave to cool slightly then gradually beat in the eggs to make a smooth, shiny paste.

3 Place the mixture in a piping bag fitted with a 1.25cm (½ in) plain pipe. Pipe 20 éclairs, each about 5cm (2 in) long, on to the baking sheets, leaving room for them to expand during cooking. Bake in the preheated oven for about 20 minutes, or until well risen and golden brown.

4 Remove from the oven and split one side of each éclair with a knife to allow the steam to escape. If the insides of the split éclairs are still moist, then return them to the oven to dry out for a further 5 minutes.

5 To make the filling, fold the icing sugar and coffee essence into the whipped cream. Pipe or spoon the cream into the middle of the base of the éclairs and replace the top.

6 To make the icing, measure the chocolate, water and butter into a heatproof bowl and heat gently over a pan of simmering water until melted. Remove from the heat and beat in the icing sugar until smooth. Pour into a shallow dish and dip each éclair into the chocolate mixture to coat the top. Allow to set on a wire rack.

# RICH CHOCOLATE TRAYBAKE

*Ideally you should ice the cake in the tin and, when set, lift out with
a palette knife.*

**MAKES 16 PIECES**

3 level tbsp cocoa
powder, sifted

3 tbsp hot water

225g (8 oz) baking
spread, from fridge

225g (8 oz) caster sugar

275g (10 oz) self-raising
flour

1 level tsp baking
powder

4 large eggs

**For the icing**

75g (3 oz) butter,
softened

50g (2 oz) cocoa powder,
sifted

225g (8 oz) icing sugar,
sifted

2 tbsp milk

1 Preheat the oven to 180°C/Fan 160°C/Gas 4. Grease a 30 x 23cm
(12 x 9 in) traybake tin and line with non-stick baking paper.

2 Blend the cocoa for the cake with the hot water in a large
bowl and leave to cool slightly. Measure all the rest of the cake
ingredients into the bowl and beat with an electric mixer until
well blended and smooth.

3 Turn the mixture into the tin and level the top. Bake in the
preheated oven for 35–40 minutes, or until the cake has shrunk
a little from the sides of the tin and springs back when pressed
in the centre with your fingertips.

4 Leave to cool in the tin.

5 To make the icing, measure all the ingredients into a large
bowl and beat well until the icing has thickened. Spread the
icing all over the traybake and leave to set.

6 Cut into 16 pieces to serve.

# WHITE CHOCOLATE AND STRAWBERRY TRAYBAKE

*When you buy freeze-dried strawberries from a supermarket, they come in 7g tubes. Use half for the cake and half for the topping.*

**MAKES 20 PIECES**

225g (8 oz) baking spread, from fridge
225g (8 oz) caster sugar
275g (10 oz) self-raising flour
1 level tsp baking powder
4 large eggs
4 tbsp milk
1 tsp vanilla extract
½ x 7g tube freeze-dried strawberries
100g (4 oz) white chocolate, melted

*For the topping*

100g (4 oz) butter, softened
175g (6 oz) icing sugar, sifted
2 tbsp milk
½ tsp vanilla extract
½ x 7g tube freeze-dried strawberries

1 Preheat the oven to 180°C/160°C Fan/Gas 4. Grease a 30 x 23cm (12 x 9 in) traybake tin and line with non-stick baking paper.

2 Measure all the traybake ingredients, except the strawberries and white chocolate, into a large bowl and beat with an electric mixer until light and fluffy. Stir in the strawberries and melted chocolate.

3 Turn the mixture into the tin and level the top. Bake in the preheated oven for 30–35 minutes, or until the cake has shrunk a little from the sides of the tin and springs back when pressed in the centre with your fingertips.

4 Leave to cool in the tin.

5 To make the icing, measure the butter, icing sugar, milk and vanilla into a bowl. Whisk until pale and creamy. Spread over the traybake and sprinkle with the strawberries.

# TOLL HOUSE COOKIES

*These biscuits are very easy to make and the children love finding the pieces of chocolate in them.*

**MAKES ABOUT 20**

100g (4 oz) butter, softened
100g (4 oz) light muscovado sugar
1 large egg
1 tsp vanilla extract
150g (5 oz) plain flour
1 level tsp baking powder
100g (4 oz) chocolate chips

**1** Preheat the oven to 190°C/Fan 170°C/Gas 5 and line two or three baking sheets with non-stick baking paper.

**2** Measure the butter and sugar into a bowl and beat well until soft and creamy. Work in all the remaining ingredients until the mixture forms a stiff dough.

**3** Divide the mixture into small pieces. Put these on the baking sheets then press flat with the palm of your hand. Bake in the preheated oven for 10–12 minutes, until they are golden brown.

**4** Leave to cool on the baking sheets for a few moments, then lift off using a palette knife and finish cooling on a wire rack.

# CHOCOLATE BISCUITS

*Lovely, light crunchy biscuits that keep well in an airtight tin.*

**MAKES 20**
100g (4 oz) butter,
    softened
50g (2 oz) caster sugar
150g (5 oz) self-raising
    flour
25g (1 oz) cocoa powder

**1** Preheat the oven to 190°C/Fan 170°C/Gas 5 and line two large baking sheets with non-stick baking paper.

**2** Measure the butter and sugar into a bowl and cream together until light. Work in the flour and cocoa. (This is done most easily by kneading the mixture together with your hands until smooth.)

**3** Take heaped teaspoonfuls of the mixture and roll it into small balls. Arrange on the prepared baking sheets, flatten down with a fork that has been dipped in cold water and bake in the preheated oven for about 10 minutes.

**4** Leave to cool on the baking sheets for a few moments, then lift off using a palette knife and finish cooling on a wire rack.

# CHOCOLATE CREAM FINGERS

*These are very similar to a well-known biscuit that is bought in shops; my family think these are far nicer and are always asking me to make them. Rolling the dough between cling film makes it easy to handle.*

**MAKES 10–12**

*For the biscuits*
100g (4 oz) plain flour
½ level tsp baking powder
2 level tbsp cocoa powder
60g (2¼ oz) butter, softened
50g (2 oz) caster sugar
1 tbsp golden syrup
2 tsp milk

*For the filling*
25g (1 oz) butter, softened
50g (2 oz) icing sugar, sifted
2 level tsp cocoa powder
a few drops vanilla extract
1 tsp milk

1 Place all the biscuit ingredients together in a bowl and beat well until they are blended and smooth. Bring the mixture together using your hands. Cover and chill in the fridge for 30 minutes.

2 Preheat the oven to 160°C/Fan 140°C/Gas 3 and line two large baking sheets with non-stick baking paper.

3 Place a sheet of cling film on the work surface and place the dough on top. Place another sheet of cling film over the dough and roll out to about 5mm (¼ in) thickness. Remove the top sheet of cling film and cut the dough into fingers about 2.5cm (1 in) wide and about 6.25cm (2½ in) long. You should get 20–24 fingers from the dough.

4 Carefully lift each finger on to a baking sheet and prick each biscuit two or three times with a fork. Bake in the preheated oven for 15–20 minutes.

5 Leave to cool on the sheets for a few moments, then lift off with a palette knife and finish cooling on a wire rack.

6 To make the filling, measure all the ingredients into a bowl and beat well until smooth and creamy. Use to sandwich the biscuits together in pairs.

# BOOZY RUM TRUFFLES

*This is a good way of using up broken biscuits and, perhaps, a stale sponge. The truffles are quick to make and require no cooking. Add trimmings of icing or marzipan, if you have them left after icing the Christmas cake. Make this recipe in two batches and keep the truffles in the fridge or store in the freezer until required.*

**MAKES 35–40**

2–3 tbsp rum

100g (4 oz) seedless raisins, finely chopped

4 tbsp apricot jam, warmed

150g (5 oz) broken plain biscuits, crushed

200g (7 oz) Madeira or sponge cake, crumbled

100g (4 oz) Bournville chocolate, melted

2 x 55g pots chocolate strands or vermicelli

1 You will need about 40 petit four cases on a baking sheet.

2 Measure the rum, raisins, jam, biscuits and cake into a large bowl. Add the melted chocolate and mix together very thoroughly until all of the mixture is covered in chocolate.

3 Shape into about 40 little truffle balls and roll each one in the chocolate vermicelli strands. Place in the petit four cases.

4 Leave to chill in the fridge for about 1 hour before eating.

CHAPTER FOUR

# FAMILY
# FRUIT
# CAKES

# EASY APPLE CAKE

*It is best to use a loose-bottomed cake or springform tin for this as it is often difficult to turn out. If you do not have one, line the base of an ordinary tin with foil or baking paper and, after allowing it to cool for 15 minutes, carefully turn out on to a flat plate. Then peel off the foil or paper and reverse the cake on to another plate.*

### SERVES 8
250g (9 oz) cooking apples (peeled weight)
175g (6 oz) self-raising flour
175g (6 oz) caster sugar, plus extra to sprinkle
2 large eggs
½ tsp almond extract
100g (4 oz) butter, melted

1 Preheat the oven to 180°C/Fan 160°C/Gas 4 and line a 20cm (8 in) loose-bottomed cake or springform tin with non-stick baking paper.

2 Thinly slice the apples and put them in a bowl of water.

3 Measure the flour into a bowl with the sugar. Beat the eggs and almond extract together and stir them into the flour, together with the melted butter, and mix well. Spread half this mixture into the tin.

4 Drain and dry the apples on kitchen paper and arrange them on the cake mixture. Top with the remaining cake mixture; it is not very easy to spread but if the apples show through it doesn't matter too much.

5 Bake in the preheated oven for 1¼ hours, or until golden and shrinking slightly from the sides of the tin.

6 Leave to cool for 15 minutes then turn out and remove the paper.

7 Sift over some caster sugar and serve warm with cream.

### VARIATION: MINI APPLE CAKES
Prepare the cake mix and apples as above. Arrange 12 muffin cases in a muffin tin. Place 1 tablespoon of the cake mix in each muffin case and top with the sliced apples. Cover with the remaining cake mixture and bake in the preheated oven for 25–30 minutes until well risen and lightly brown.

# SPECIAL APRICOT CAKE

*Utterly delicious. A can of apricots is added to this cake and gives it its distinctive flavour. Use the juice from the can in a fruit salad or soak sponge cakes in it for a trifle. I've added a small bake version – these are lovely served warm.*

**SERVES 6–8**
100g (4 oz) baking
    spread, from fridge
100g (4 oz) light
    muscovado sugar
2 large eggs
¼ tsp almond extract
200g (7 oz) self-raising
    flour
½ level tsp baking
    powder
1 x 240g can apricot
    halves, drained
    and chopped
200g (7 oz) mixed
    dried fruit

1 Preheat the oven to 160°C/Fan 140°C/Gas 3. Grease a 17.5cm (7 in) round cake tin and line with non-stick baking paper.

2 Measure all the ingredients except the fruit into a large mixing bowl and beat with an electric mixer until well blended. Stir in the apricots and dried fruit.

3 Turn the mixture into the tin and level the top. Bake in the preheated oven for 1½ hours, or until the cake is golden brown. A skewer inserted into the centre of the cake should come out clean.

4 Leave to cool in the tin for 10 minutes then turn out, remove the paper and leave to cool on a wire rack.

## VARIATION: MINI APRICOT CAKES
Prepare the cake mix as above and use to fill 12 muffin cases set in a muffin tin. Cook for 25–30 minutes at 180°C/Fan 160°C/Gas 4 until well risen and lightly brown. Serve warm.

# PINEAPPLE UPSIDE-DOWN CAKE

*This cake always looks and tastes good and is delicious if served warm at a coffee morning.*

**SERVES 6–8**

*For the cake*
75g (3 oz) self-raising flour
75g (3 oz) baking spread, from fridge
75g (3 oz) caster sugar
1 large egg, beaten
1 tbsp pineapple juice

*For the topping*
50g (2 oz) light muscovado sugar
1 x 227g can pineapple slices, drained
2 glacé cherries, halved

1 Preheat the oven to 190°C/Fan 170°C/Gas 5 and thoroughly grease a 17.5cm (7 in) round cake tin (don't use a tin with a removable base or the syrup will leak through).

2 Measure all the cake ingredients into a bowl and beat with an electric mixer until well blended.

3 Sprinkle the brown sugar in the bottom of the tin and place 4 pineapple rings on top. Add a halved cherry in the centre of each ring then carefully spread the cake mixture over the pineapples and level the top.

4 Bake in the preheated oven for about 25 minutes, or until well risen and golden brown and the centre springs back when lightly pressed with your fingertips.

5 Leave to cool for about 20 minutes in the tin then turn out on to a serving plate.

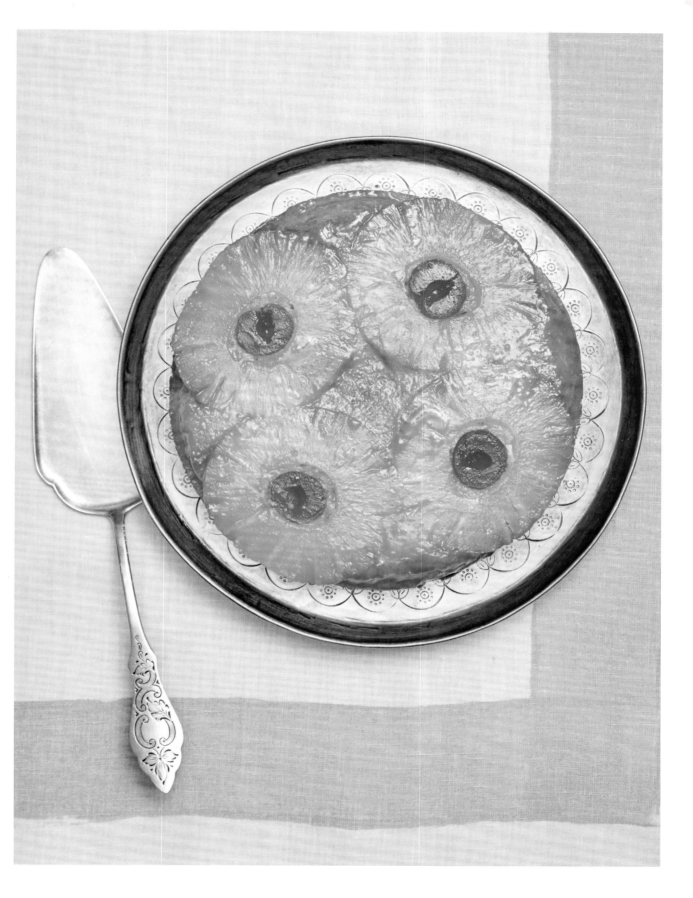

# PINEAPPLE AND RAISIN CAKE

*This is a less rich, moist kind of Christmas cake. It is best made just before Christmas, kept cool and eaten within a month – store in a plastic container in the fridge. Drain the pineapple very well and keep the juice for a fruit salad or trifle. I've added a small bake version for when you want a quick fruity cupcake.*

**SERVES 8**

1 x 227g can pineapple (chunks, rings or crushed), excluding the juice
150g (5 oz) butter, softened
100g (4 oz) light muscovado sugar
2 large eggs
200g (7 oz) self-raising flour
2 tbsp milk
400g (14 oz) seedless raisins

1 Preheat the oven to 160°C/Fan 140°C/Gas 3. Grease a 20cm (8 in) round cake tin and line with non-stick baking paper.

2 Drain and chop the pineapple very finely then dry on kitchen paper.

3 Cream the butter and sugar together in a mixing bowl. Beat in the eggs, adding a tablespoon of flour with the last egg. Fold in the flour and stir in the milk and, last of all, the fruit, including the pineapple.

4 Turn into the tin, place in the centre of the preheated oven and bake for about 2 hours, or until the cake is a pale golden brown and shrinking away from the sides of the tin.

5 Leave to cool in the tin then remove the paper to serve or store in an airtight tin.

---

**VARIATION: MINI PINEAPPLE AND RAISIN CAKES**
Preheat the oven to 180°C/Fan 160°C/Gas 4 and arrange 12 muffin cases in a muffin tin. Using 225g (8 oz) of raisins instead of 400g (14 oz), measure all the ingredients into a large mixing bowl and beat with an electric mixer until well blended. Spoon into the paper cases and cook for 25–30 minutes, or until well risen and lightly brown. Serve warm.

# SPECIAL CHERRY CAKE

*A classic cake. It is important to cut the cherries up and then wash and dry them thoroughly so that all moisture is removed.*

**SERVES 8**

175g (6 oz) glacé
  cherries
225g (8 oz) self-raising
  flour
175g (6 oz) baking
  spread, from fridge
175g (6 oz) caster sugar
finely grated zest
  of 1 lemon
50g (2 oz) ground
  almonds
3 large eggs

**1** Preheat the oven to 160°C/Fan 140°C/Gas 3. Grease a 20cm (8 in) round cake tin and line with non-stick baking paper.

**2** Cut each cherry into quarters, put in a sieve and rinse under running water. Drain well and dry very thoroughly on absorbent kitchen paper.

**3** Place all the remaining ingredients in a large bowl and beat with an electric mixer until well blended. Lightly fold in the cherries. The mixture will be fairly stiff which will help to keep the cherries evenly suspended in the cake while it is baking.

**4** Turn into the tin and bake in the preheated oven for about 1¼ hours, or until a skewer inserted into the centre of the cake comes out clean.

**5** Leave to cool in the tin for 10 minutes then turn out and finish cooling on a wire rack.

**6** Store in an airtight tin.

# MINCEMEAT CAKE

*This is a very light, moist fruit cake and is quite delicious. This small bake version takes only 25–30 minutes in the oven and would make a lovely alternative to Christmas cake in the festive season.*

**SERVES 10**

150g (5 oz) baking spread, from fridge
150g (5 oz) light muscovado sugar
2 large eggs
225g (8 oz) self-raising flour
75g (3 oz) sultanas
225g (8 oz) mincemeat
25g (1 oz) flaked almonds

**1** Preheat the oven to 160°C/Fan 140°C/Gas 3. Grease a 20cm (8 in) round cake tin and line with non-stick baking paper.

**2** Measure the baking spread, sugar, eggs and flour into a large bowl and beat with an electric mixer until well blended. Stir in the sultanas and mincemeat.

**3** Turn the mixture into the tin, level the top and sprinkle over the almonds. Bake in the preheated oven for about 1¾ hours, or until golden brown and shrinking away from the sides of the tin.

**4** Leave to cool in the tin then remove the paper to serve or store in an airtight tin.

**VARIATION: MINI MINCEMEAT CAKES**
Preheat the oven to 180°C/Fan 160°C/Gas 4 and arrange 12 muffin cases in a muffin tin. Using 175g (6 oz) of mincemeat instead of 225g (8 oz), measure all the ingredients, except the almonds, into a large mixing bowl and beat with a wooden spoon until well blended. Spoon into the paper cases, sprinkle with the flaked almonds and bake for 25–30 minutes, or until well risen and lightly brown. Cool on a wire rack.

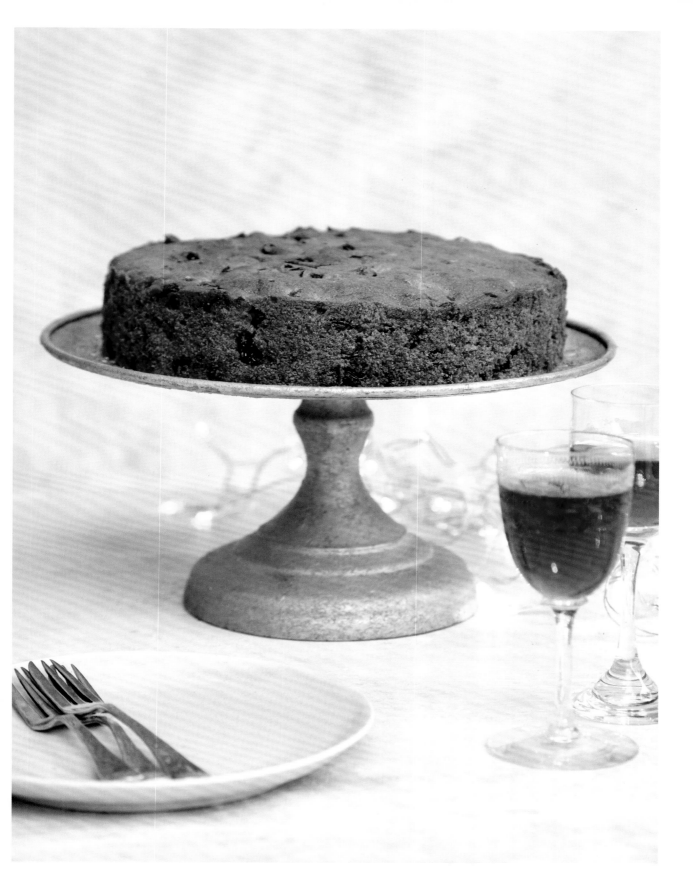

# FRUGAL CAKE

*A basic and easy family fruit cake that can be made with any dried fruit you have in the cupboard. It's best eaten on the day it is made.*

**SERVES 8**

225g (8 oz) self-raising flour
100g (4 oz) baking spread, from fridge
100g (4 oz) light muscovado sugar
2 large eggs
3 tbsp milk
225g (8 oz) mixed dried fruit
1 level tbsp demerara sugar

**1** Preheat the oven to 180°C/Fan 160°C/Gas 4. Grease a 17.5cm (7 in) deep round cake tin and line with non-stick baking paper.

**2** Measure all the ingredients, except the dried fruit and demerara sugar, into a large mixing bowl and beat with an electric mixer until well blended. Stir in the dried fruit.

**3** Turn the mixture into the tin, level the top and sprinkle with the demerara sugar. Bake in the preheated oven for about 1 hour, or until a skewer inserted into the centre of the cake comes out clean.

**4** Leave to cool in the tin for about 30 minutes, then turn out, remove the paper and finish cooling on a wire rack.

# BANANA AND CHOCOLATE CHIP MUFFINS

*Banana and chocolate is a great combination and these American-style muffins go down really well with children. They are also very easy to make.*

**MAKES 12**

2 ripe bananas, mashed with a fork (about 200g/7 oz)
250g (9 oz) self-raising flour
1 level tsp baking powder
100g (4 oz) baking spread, from fridge
175g (6 oz) light muscovado sugar
2 large eggs
1 x 150g pot natural yoghurt
2 tbsp milk
100g (4 oz) dark chocolate chips

1 Preheat the oven to 180°C/Fan 160°C/Gas 4 and arrange 12 muffin cases in a muffin tin.

2 Measure all the ingredients except the chocolate chips into a large mixing bowl and beat with an electric mixer until well blended. Stir in the chocolate chips.

3 Spoon into the muffin cases and bake in the preheated oven for about 25–30 minutes, until well risen and lightly golden brown.

4 Lift off and leave to cool on a wire rack.

# MINI FRUIT CUPCAKES

*If you don't have time to bake a fruit cake, try this recipe. Here we've taken the basic fruit cake mix and turned it into a really quick bake.*

**MAKES 12**

100g (4 oz) butter,
  softened
100g (4 oz) caster sugar
finely grated zest
  of 1 small orange
2 large eggs
½ level tsp ground
  ginger
100g (4 oz) self-raising
  flour
175g (6 oz) mixed
  dried fruit
25g (1 oz) glacé cherries,
  chopped, rinsed and
  thoroughly dried

1 Preheat the oven to 180°C/Fan 160°C/Gas 4 and arrange 12 fairy cake paper cases in a muffin tin.

2 Measure all the ingredients except the mixed fruit and cherries, into a large bowl and beat with an electric mixer until light, fluffy and well blended. Stir in the fruit and cherries.

3 Spoon into the paper cases and bake in the preheated oven for about 25 minutes, or until well risen and lightly golden brown.

4 Cool on a wire rack.

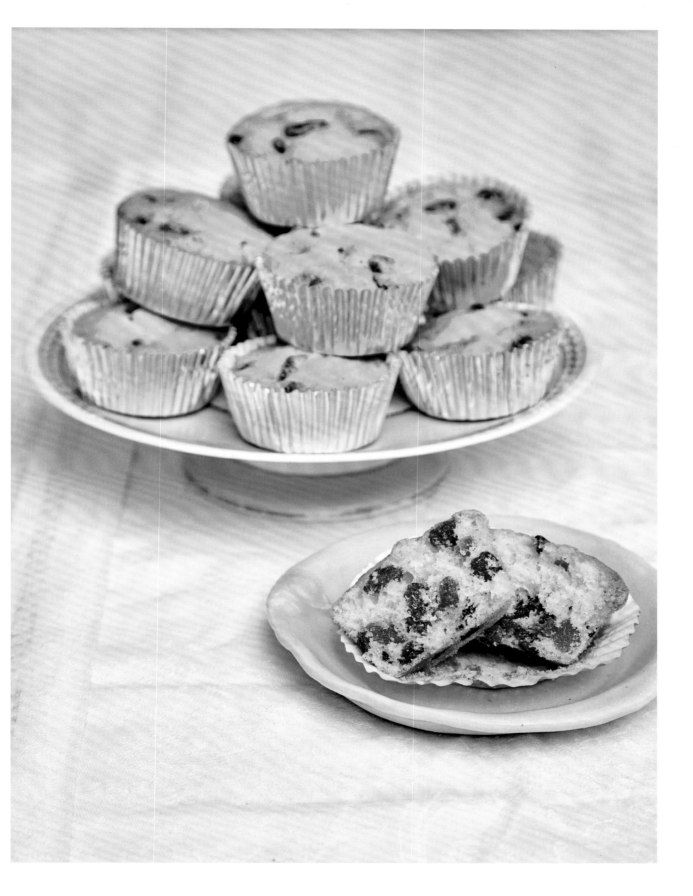

# VICARAGE FRUIT CAKE

*This cake keeps very well if you wrap it in foil or store it in an airtight tin. It is a moist fruit cake and is ideal to cut and include in a lunch box or to take on a picnic.*

**SERVES 8**

1 x 397g can full-fat condensed milk
150g (5 oz) baking spread, from fridge
225g (8 oz) seedless raisins
225g (8 oz) sultanas
225g (8 oz) currants
100g (4 oz) glacé cherries, chopped, rinsed and thoroughly dried
225g (8 oz) plain flour
2 level tsp ground mixed spice
1 level tsp ground cinnamon
½ level tsp bicarbonate of soda
2 large eggs

**1** Preheat the oven to 150°C/Fan 130°C/Gas 2. Grease a 17.5cm (7 in) round cake tin and line with non-stick baking paper.

**2** Pour the condensed milk into a heavy-based saucepan, add the spread, fruit and glacé cherries. Place over a low heat until the spread has melted. Stir well and warm through for 5 minutes, stirring regularly so the condensed milk doesn't catch.

**3** Remove from the heat and leave on one side to cool for about 10 minutes, stirring occasionally to help speed up this process.

**4** Meanwhile, sift the flour, spices and bicarbonate of soda into a large bowl and make a well in the centre. Add the eggs and the cooled fruit mixture and mix together quickly until well blended.

**5** Turn the mixture into the tin, level the top and bake in the preheated oven for 1¾–2 hours, or until well risen. A skewer inserted into the centre of the cake should come out clean.

**6** Leave to cool in the tin for about 10 minutes then turn out and leave to finish cooling on a wire rack.

# DUNDEE CAKE

*All the better for keeping for a week or so.*

**SERVES 12**

150g (5 oz) butter, softened
150g (5 oz) light muscovado sugar
3 large eggs
250g (9 oz) plain flour
1 level tsp baking powder
175g (6 oz) sultanas
75g (3 oz) currants
75g (3 oz) seedless raisins
50g (2 oz) glacé cherries, halved, rinsed and thoroughly dried
50g (2 oz) mixed candied peel, chopped
2 level tbsp ground almonds
finely grated zest of 1 large lemon
50g (2 oz) blanched almonds, halved, to decorate

**1** Preheat the oven to 160°C/Fan 140°C/Gas 3. Grease a 20cm (8 in) loose-bottomed cake or springform tin and line with non-stick baking paper.

**2** Measure the butter, sugar, eggs, flour and baking powder into a large bowl and beat with an electric mixer until well blended. Stir in the fruit, peel, ground almonds and lemon zest.

**3** Spoon the mixture into the cake tin and smooth the top. Arrange the almonds in circles over the top of the cake and bake in the preheated oven for about 1½ hours, or until a deep golden brown. A warm skewer inserted into the centre of the cake should come out clean. Cover the cake with foil halfway through baking if it is browning too quickly.

**4** Leave to cool in the tin for about 20 minutes then turn out, remove the paper and finish cooling on a wire rack.

# FAMILY FRUIT CAKE

*This cake improves with keeping and is the ideal cake to bake a week
in advance and take away on a self-catering holiday or weekend.*

**SERVES 10**

225g (8 oz) butter,
    softened
225g (8 oz) caster sugar
finely grated zest of
    1 orange
4 large eggs
1 level tsp ground
    ginger
225g (8 oz) self-raising
    flour
350g (12 oz) mixed
    dried fruit
50g (2 oz) glacé cherries,
    quartered, rinsed and
    thoroughly dried

1 Preheat the oven to 160°C/Fan 140°C/Gas 3. Grease a 20cm
(8 in) deep round cake tin and line with non-stick baking paper.

2 Measure the butter, sugar, orange zest, eggs, ginger and flour
into a large bowl. Beat with an electric mixer until light, fluffy
and well blended. Stir in the mixed fruit and cherries.

3 Turn the mixture into the tin, level the top and bake in the
preheated oven for about 2–2½ hours, or until the middle feels
firm to the touch. A skewer inserted into the centre of the cake
should come out clean.

4 Leave to cool in the tin then remove the paper to store
in an airtight tin.

# EASTER SIMNEL CAKE

*The traditional Easter cake.*

**SERVES 10**

175g (6 oz) baking
  spread, from fridge
175g (6 oz) light
  muscovado sugar
3 large eggs
175g (6 oz) self-raising
  flour
2 level tsp ground
  mixed spice
2 tbsp milk
275g (10 oz) mixed
  dried fruit
50g (2 oz) glacé cherries,
  halved, rinsed and
  thoroughly dried
finely grated zest of
  1 orange or lemon
50g (2 oz) ground
  almonds

*For the decoration*
450g (1 lb) golden
  marzipan
1 tbsp apricot jam,
  sieved
1 large egg white,
  beaten with a fork

1 Preheat the oven to 160°C/Fan 140°C/Gas 3. Grease a 17.5cm (7 in) deep round cake tin and line with non-stick baking paper.

2 Measure all the cake ingredients into a large mixing bowl and beat together with a wooden spoon until well blended – this will take 2–3 minutes.

3 Place half the cake mixture in the bottom of the tin and level the top.

4 Take one-third of the marzipan and roll out to a circle the size of the tin then place on top of the cake mixture. Cover with the remaining cake mixture and level the top.

5 Bake in the preheated oven for about 2¼ hours, or until a skewer inserted into the centre of the cake comes out clean.

6 Turn out, remove the paper and leave to cool on a wire rack.

7 Brush the top of the cooled cake with the jam then roll half the remaining marzipan into a circle to fit the top of the cake. Press in place and pinch the edges to crimp decoratively.

8 Roll out the remaining marzipan and shape into 11 small balls. Arrange around the edge of the cake. Using a sharp knife, score the centre of the marzipan in a crisscross pattern. Brush with a little egg white and put under a preheated grill for 3–4 minutes to brown lightly. Leave to cool.

# VICTORIAN CHRISTMAS CAKE

*An easy and special Christmas cake. The fruit is soaked for three days, which makes it very moist. This is not a deep cake so don't expect it to rise to the top of the tin.*

**SERVES 12**

175g (6 oz) seedless raisins, chopped
500g (1 lb 2 oz) currants
350g (12 oz) sultanas
350g (12 oz) glacé cherries, quartered, rinsed and thoroughly dried
150ml (¼ pint) medium or sweet sherry
finely grated zest of 2 oranges
250g (9 oz) butter, softened
250g (9 oz) light muscovado sugar
4 large eggs
1 tbsp black treacle
75g (3 oz) blanched almonds, chopped
75g (3 oz) self-raising flour
175g (6 oz) plain flour
1½ level tsp ground mixed spice
450g (1 lb) marzipan or almond paste (see opposite)
3 tbsp apricot jam, warmed
675g (1½ lb) royal icing (see opposite)

**1** Put the fruit and cherries in a container, pour over the sherry and stir in the orange zest. Cover with a lid and leave to soak for at least 3 days, stirring daily.

**2** Preheat the oven to 140°C/Fan 120°C/Gas 1. Grease a 23cm (9 in) deep round cake tin and line with non-stick baking paper.

**3** Measure the butter, sugar, eggs, treacle and almonds into a very large bowl and beat well with a wooden spoon. Sift together the flours and spice and add to the bowl. Mix together until well blended. Stir in the soaked fruit and sherry.

**4** Turn the mixture into the tin and level the top. Bake in the centre of the preheated oven for 4–4½ hours, or until firm to the touch and a rich golden brown. Check after 2 hours and if the cake is the perfect colour, cover with foil for the remainder of the cooking. A skewer inserted into the centre of the cake should come out clean.

**5** Leave to cool in the tin.

**6** Liberally dust a work surface with icing sugar and roll out the marzipan to about 5cm (2 in) larger than the surface of the cake. Brush the cake with apricot jam then carefully lift the marzipan over the cake. Gently level and smooth with the rolling pin, easing the almond paste down the sides of the cake.

**7** Spread the icing evenly over the top and sides of the cake with a palette knife. Leave the cake loosely covered overnight for the icing to harden a little.

# ALMOND PASTE

*To cover a 23cm (9 in) round cake.*

150g (5 oz) icing sugar
250g (9 oz) ground
    almonds
150g (5 oz) caster sugar
1 large egg
1 tsp almond extract

**1** Sift the icing sugar into a bowl, add the ground almonds and sugar and mix well.

**2** Add the egg and almond extract then work the mixture into a small smooth ball by hand – but do not over knead.

**3** Wrap in cling film and store in the fridge until required.


# ROYAL ICING

*To cover a 23cm (9 in) round cake.*

3 large egg whites
675g (1½ lb) icing sugar,
    sifted
3 tsp lemon juice
1½ tsp glycerine

**1** Whisk the egg whites in a large bowl until they become frothy.

**2** Add the icing sugar, a spoonful at a time, then add the lemon juice and glycerine. Beat the icing until it is very stiff and white and will stand up in peaks.

**3** Cover the surface of the icing tightly with cling film and keep in a cool place until needed.

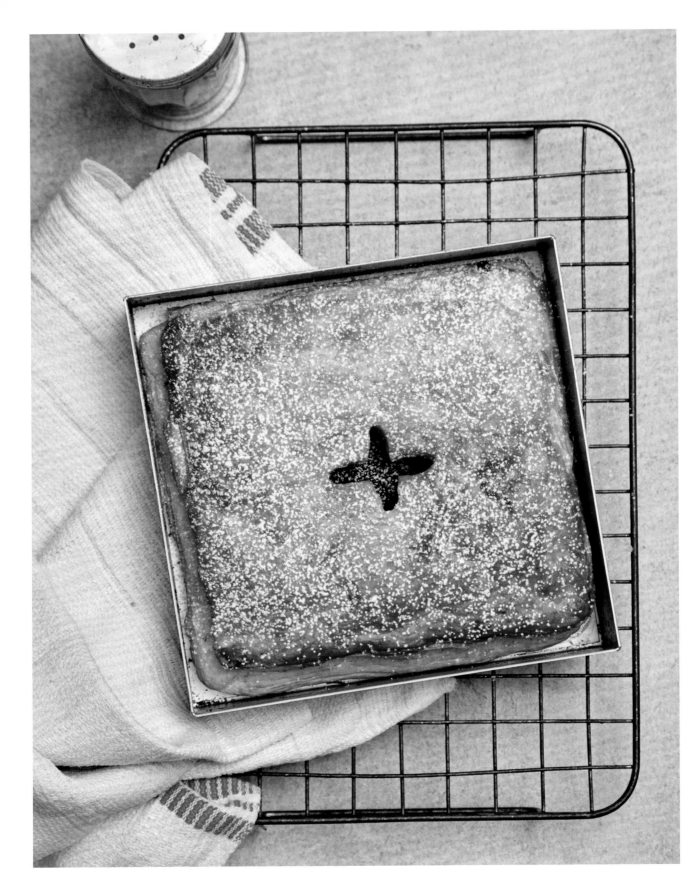

# BANBURY TART

*Although I live near Banbury, I have never managed to buy a Banbury cake there; I am told that they take too long to make. So I make it myself and it takes no time at all!*

**SERVES 8**
25g (1 oz) butter
15g (½ oz) plain flour
150g (5 oz) currants
50g (2 oz) light
   muscovado sugar
a little grated nutmeg
2 tbsp sherry or rum
½ x 500g packet
   puff pastry
a little milk, to glaze
icing sugar, to dust

1 Preheat the oven to 220°C/Fan 200°C/Gas 7.

2 To make the filling, melt the butter in a saucepan over a gentle heat and stir in the flour. Cook for 1 minute. Remove from the heat and add the currants, sugar, nutmeg and sherry or rum, mix well then leave to cool.

3 Meanwhile, cut the pastry in half. Roll out one piece and use it to line the base and sides of a 17.5cm (7 in) square tin. Spread with the filling.

4 Roll out the remaining pastry, damp the edges then cover the fruit with this pastry lid. Seal the edges well and firmly, brush the top with a little milk and make two cuts in the centre of the pie.

5 Bake in the preheated oven for about 25 minutes, or until the pastry has risen and is golden brown.

6 Leave to cool in the tin then dust with icing sugar before serving.

# DATE AND WALNUT CAKE

*This is a cake with a lovely flavour. It is ideal to include in a packed lunch and it keeps very well.*

**MAKES 16 SQUARES**

200ml (7 fl oz) boiling water
175g (6 oz) semi-dried Medjool dates, stoned and chopped
¾ level tsp bicarbonate of soda
50g (2 oz) butter, softened
175g (6 oz) light muscovado sugar
1 small egg, beaten
225g (8 oz) plain flour
¾ level tsp baking powder
50g (2 oz) walnuts, chopped

1 Preheat the oven to 180°C/Fan 160°C/Gas 4. Grease a 20cm (8 in) square cake tin and line with non-stick baking paper.

2 Measure the water, dates and bicarbonate of soda into a bowl and leave to stand for 5 minutes.

3 Cream the butter and sugar together then beat in the egg, together with the water and date mixture.

4 Sift the flour with the baking powder and salt and fold into the fruit mixture, together with the walnuts.

5 Turn the mixture into the tin, level the top and bake in the preheated oven for about 1 hour. A skewer inserted into the centre of the cake should come out clean.

6 Turn out, remove the paper and leave to cool on a wire rack. Cut into 16 squares to serve.

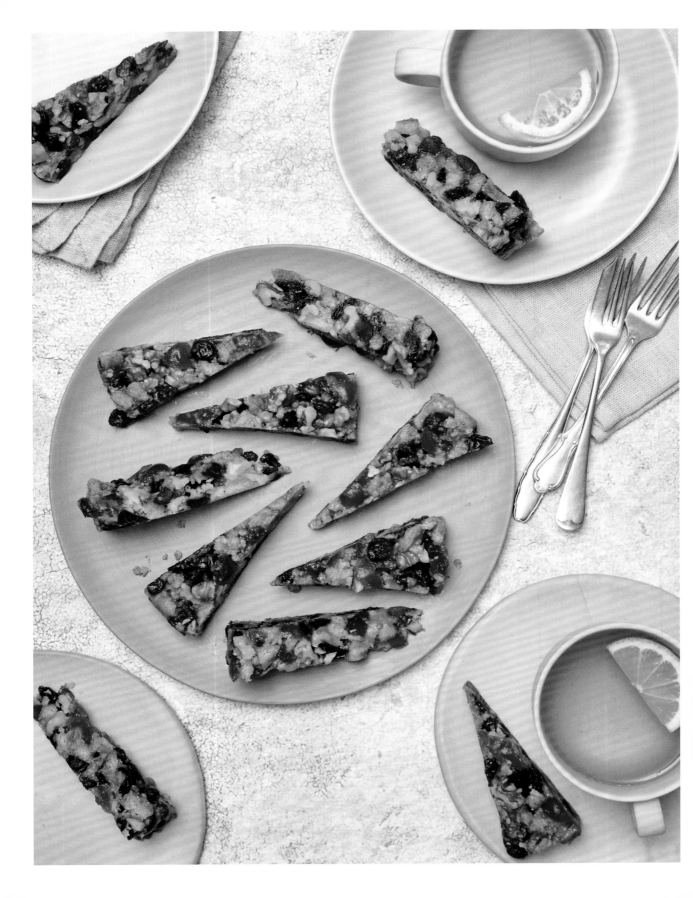

# FRUIT AND NUT FRIDGE CAKE

*This cake needs about 4 hours in the fridge to set, and it's rather rich –
so only serve in thin slices!*

**MAKES 16 SLICES**

175g (6 oz) unsalted butter

4 heaped tbsp golden syrup

100g (4 oz) glacé cherries, chopped, rinsed and thoroughly dried

100g (4 oz) dried dates, stoned and chopped

100g (4 oz) seedless raisins

100g (4 oz) walnuts, roughly chopped

225g (8 oz) digestive biscuits, broken into large crumbs

**1** Line a 20cm (8 in) loose-bottomed cake or springform tin with non-stick baking paper.

**2** Measure the butter and golden syrup into a heavy pan and heat gently until the butter has melted. Increase the heat and boil for about 3 minutes, stirring all the time. Remove from the heat and leave on one side to cool.

**3** Place all the remaining ingredients in a large bowl and pour over the cooled sauce. Mix well until evenly coated.

**4** Turn the mixture into the tin and leave to chill in the fridge for about 4 hours, until set.

**5** Turn out and cut into thin slices to serve.

CHAPTER FIVE

# LITTLE CAKES, BUNS AND PASTRIES

# SIMPLE QUEEN CAKES

*From this basic mixture a variety of other small cakes can be made. You could add 25g (1 oz) currants for Currant Queen Cakes or 25g (1 oz) cocoa for Chocolate Queen Cakes. The number of cases required will vary slightly if the cakes are to be iced (see Iced Queen Cakes on page 164) or extra ingredients added. Make sure you stand the paper cases in a bun tin as it helps to keep them in a good shape and prevents them toppling over.*

**MAKES 12**

150g (5 oz) baking spread, from fridge
150g (5 oz) caster sugar
150g (5 oz) self-raising flour
3 large eggs
1 level tsp baking powder

1 Preheat the oven to 200°C/Fan 180°C/Gas 6 and arrange 12 muffin cases in a muffin tin.

2 Measure all the ingredients into a large mixing bowl and beat with an electric mixer until well blended and smooth.

3 Divide the mixture between the paper cases and bake in the preheated oven for about 20 minutes, or until the cakes are well risen and golden brown.

4 Lift out and cool on a wire rack.

# ICED ORANGE QUEEN CAKES

*Make sure that you do not fill the cases too full – leave about 1cm (½ in) between the mixture and the top of the paper case before baking. You could also make these cakes using lemon zest and lemon juice instead.*

**MAKES 24**
100g (4 oz) baking
 spread, from fridge
100g (4 oz) caster sugar
100g (4 oz) self-raising
 flour
2 large eggs
½ level tsp baking
 powder
finely grated zest of
 1 small orange

*For the icing*
juice of 1 small orange
375g (13 oz) icing sugar

**1** Preheat the oven to 200°C/Fan 180°C/Gas 6 and arrange 24 fairy cake paper cases in two bun tins.

**2** Measure all the cake ingredients into a large mixing bowl and beat with an electric mixer until well blended and smooth.

**3** Divide the mixture between the paper cases – do not over fill as you need a little of the rim of the paper case above the level of the cakes when they are baked so that it is easy to ice the top. Bake in the preheated oven for about 15 minutes, or until the cakes are well risen and golden brown.

**4** Lift out and cool on a wire rack.

**5** Use the juice to make a little glacé icing with the icing sugar. Add a little bit of water, if necessary, to give a smooth coating consistency. Spoon over the top of the cakes and decorate as liked.

# ICED QUEEN CAKES

*When you ice the cakes, the icing should cover the top and touch the edge of the cases. If you want to have a variety of colours, divide the icing into separate bowls once it has been made and then colour each one as desired. Depending on the size of your cases, you will have between 18 and 24 cakes.*

**MAKES 18–24**
100g (4 oz) baking
  spread, from fridge
100g (4 oz) caster sugar
100g (4 oz) self-raising
  flour
2 large eggs
½ level tsp baking
  powder

*For the icing*
375g (13 oz) icing sugar
decorations, as liked

**1** Preheat the oven to 200°C/Fan 180°C/Gas 6 and arrange 24 fairy cake paper cases in two bun tins.

**2** Place all the cake ingredients into a large mixing bowl and beat with an electric mixer until well blended and smooth.

**3** Divide the mixture between the paper cases – leave about 1cm (½ in) between the mixture and the top of the paper cases. It is important not over fill the cases as you need a little of the rim of the paper case above the level of the cakes when they are baked so that it is easy to ice the top. Bake in the preheated oven for about 15 minutes, or until the cakes are well risen and golden brown.

**4** Lift out and cool on a wire rack.

**5** To make the icing, mix the icing sugar with 3–4 tablespoons of water to give a smooth coating consistency. Spoon over the cakes and decorate as liked.

# COFFEE BUNS

*By adding coffee to the basic queen cake recipe, you have a lovely variation on the original.*

**MAKES 12**

1½ level tsp instant coffee granules
3 large eggs
150g (5 oz) baking spread, from fridge
150g (5 oz) caster sugar
150g (5 oz) self-raising flour
1 level tsp baking powder

*For the icing*

50g (2 oz) butter, softened
150g (5 oz) icing sugar, sifted
2 tsp coffee essence

1 Preheat the oven to 200°C/Fan 180°C/Gas 6 and arrange 12 muffin cases in a muffin tin.

2 Dissolve the coffee granules in the eggs and then measure all the cake ingredients into a large mixing bowl and beat with an electric mixer until well blended and smooth.

3 Divide the mixture between the paper cases and bake in the preheated oven for about 20 minutes, or until the cakes are well risen and golden brown.

4 Lift out and cool on a wire rack.

5 To make the icing, blend the butter with the icing sugar and coffee essence. Spread a little icing on the top of each cake so that the top is completely covered.

# TREACLE SPICE BUNS

*These are quick to make and bake and are best eaten warm, straight from the oven.*

**MAKES 12**

50g (2 oz) black treacle
50g (2 oz) baking
  spread, from fridge
175g (6 oz) self-raising
  flour
75g (3 oz) sultanas
75g (3 oz) light
  muscovado sugar
1 level tsp ground
  cinnamon
½ level tsp baking
  powder
1 large egg

**1** Preheat the oven to 200°C/Fan 180°C/Gas 6 and arrange 12 fairy cake paper cases in a bun tin.

**2** Measure the treacle and spread into a small saucepan and heat gently until the spread has melted. Remove from the heat and cool slightly.

**3** Measure all the remaining ingredients into a bowl, stir in the treacle mixture and mix thoroughly.

**4** Divide the mixture between the paper cases and bake in the preheated oven for about 15–20 minutes, or until the buns are well risen and cooked.

**5** Leave to cool in the tins for a few minutes then lift out and serve while they are still warm – fresh from the oven.

# BUTTERFLY CAKES

*These little cakes are a classic and are a lovely alternative to a standard queen cake. You could flavour them with orange or lemon zest, or make coffee butterfly cakes by adding coffee essence to the basic mixture. These will have a better domed shape if they are cooked in a shallow bun tin, rather than a high-sided muffin tin.*

**MAKES 12**
100g (4 oz) baking
  spread, from fridge
100g (4 oz) caster sugar
100g (4 oz) self-raising
  flour
2 large eggs
½ level tsp baking
  powder

*For the icing*
75g (3 oz) butter,
  softened
150g (5 oz) icing sugar,
  sifted, plus extra
  to dust

1 Preheat the oven to 200°C/Fan 180°C/Gas 6 and arrange 12 fairy cake paper cases in a bun tin.

2 Measure all of the cake ingredients into a large mixing bowl and beat with an electric mixer until well blended and smooth.

3 Divide the mixture between the paper cases and bake in the preheated oven for about 15 minutes, or until the cakes are well risen and golden brown.

4 Lift out and cool on a wire rack.

5 To make the icing, beat the butter and icing sugar together until well blended and smooth.

6 Cut a slice from the top of each cake and cut this slice in half. Pipe a swirl of butter icing in the centre of each cake and then replace the two half slices of cake into the icing, butterfly fashion. Dust with icing sugar before serving.

# LEMON AND CHERRY BUNS

*These are the sort of small cakes that are ideal to give as a contribution for a coffee morning.*

**MAKES 12**
50g (2 oz) baking
    spread, from fridge
50g (2 oz) caster sugar
1 large egg, beaten
75g (3 oz) self-raising
    flour
50g (2 oz) semolina
½ level tsp baking
    powder
finely grated zest
    of 1 lemon
3 tbsp milk

**For the topping**
75g (3 oz) icing sugar,
    sifted
juice of about ½ lemon
6 glacé cherries, halved

1 Preheat the oven to 190°C/Fan 170°C/Gas 5 and arrange 12 fairy cake paper cases in a bun tin.

2 Measure all the cake ingredients into a mixing bowl and beat with an electric mixer until well blended.

3 Divide the mixture between the paper cases and bake in the preheated oven for about 15 minutes, or until risen and golden brown.

4 Lift out and cool on a wire rack.

5 To make the topping, mix the icing sugar with sufficient lemon juice to give a spreading consistency. Spread a little on top of each bun and decorate with a cherry.

# MOCHA BUNS

*I always stand the paper cases in a bun tin so that the buns keep a good round shape.*

**MAKES 12**

100g (4 oz) self-raising flour
½ level tsp baking powder
25g (1 oz) semolina
75g (3 oz) baking spread, from fridge
50g (2 oz) caster sugar
1 large egg, beaten
3 tbsp milk
1 tbsp coffee essence

**For the icing**

40g (1½ oz) butter, softened
25g (1 oz) cocoa powder, sifted
about 2 tbsp milk
100g (4 oz) icing sugar, sifted

1 Preheat the oven to 190°C/Fan 170°C/Gas 5 and arrange 12 fairy cake paper cases in a bun tin.

2 Measure all the bun ingredients into a mixing bowl and beat with an electric mixer until well blended and smooth.

3 Divide the mixture between the paper cases and bake in the preheated oven for about 15 minutes, or until well risen.

4 Lift out and cool on a wire rack.

5 To make the icing, measure all the ingredients into a bowl and beat well until smooth. Spread a little on top of each bun then leave to set.

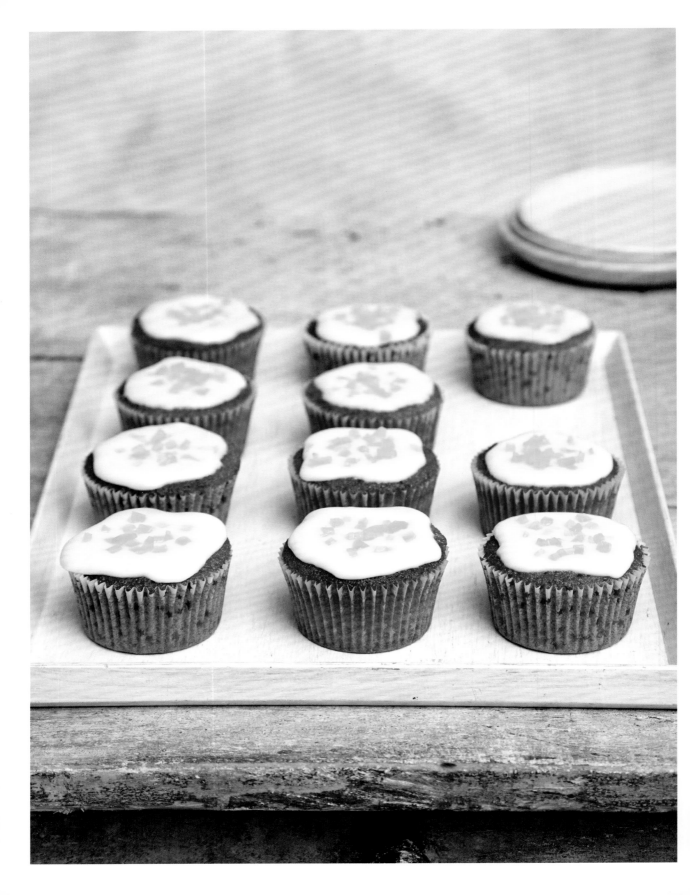

# STICKY GINGER BUNS

*These ginger buns – the stem ginger and golden syrup give them a lovely flavour – are best eaten on the day they are made.*

**MAKES 12**
100g (4 oz) self-raising flour
100g (4 oz) baking spread, from fridge
75g (3 oz) caster sugar
2 tbsp golden syrup
1 level tsp baking powder
2 level tsp ground ginger
2 large eggs

**For the icing**
225g (8 oz) icing sugar, sifted
1 tbsp water
about 2 tbsp ginger syrup from the jar (see below)
25g (1 oz) stem ginger, drained and finely chopped

1 Preheat the oven to 180°C/Fan 160°C/Gas 4 and arrange 12 fairy cake paper cases in a bun tin.

2 Measure all the bun ingredients into a large mixing bowl and beat with an electric mixer until thoroughly blended.

3 Divide the mixture between the paper cases and bake in the preheated oven for about 15–20 minutes, or until golden brown.

4 Lift out and cool on a wire rack.

5 To make the icing, measure the icing sugar into a bowl and work in the water and sufficient syrup to give a smooth glacé icing. Spread a little on the top of each bun and allow to set. Decorate with the chopped ginger pieces.

# PINEAPPLE BUNS

*These are best eaten on the day they are prepared, otherwise the pineapple on top of the buns will lose its shine.*

**MAKES 12**

1 x 227g can pineapple slices
50g (2 oz) baking spread, from fridge
2 large eggs
100g (4 oz) caster sugar
175g (6 oz) self-raising flour
½ level tsp baking powder
1 tbsp milk

*For the icing*
100g (4 oz) icing sugar, sifted

1 Preheat the oven to 180°C/Fan 160°C/Gas 4 and arrange 12 muffin cases in a muffin tin.

2 Drain the can of pineapple, reserving the juice and one of the slices for decoration.

3 Finely chop the remaining pineapple, drain well on kitchen paper and then put in a bowl with the remaining bun ingredients. Beat well with an electric mixer until thoroughly blended.

4 Divide the mixture between the paper cases and bake in the preheated oven for about 20–25 minutes, or until golden brown.

5 Lift out and cool on a wire rack.

6 To make the icing, measure the icing sugar into a bowl and mix with sufficient pineapple juice to give a smooth spreading consistency (about 2 teaspoons). Spread a little icing on to each bun. Cut the reserved pineapple slice into 12 pieces and use to decorate the buns.

# PEPPERMINT CREAM CAKES

*Don't be over generous with the peppermint extract – 3 drops are just enough to give the icing a delicate peppermint flavour.*

**MAKES 12**

1 level tbsp cocoa powder
1 tbsp hot water
100g (4 oz) baking spread, from fridge
100g (4 oz) caster sugar
100g (4 oz) self-raising flour
1 level tsp baking powder
2 large eggs

*For the topping*

225g (8 oz) icing sugar, sifted
about 2 tbsp cold water
2–3 drops peppermint extract
2–3 drops green colouring
chocolate peppermints or chocolate mint balls, to decorate (optional)

1 Preheat the oven to 180°C/Fan 160°C/Gas 4 and arrange 12 fairy cake paper cases in a bun tin.

2 Measure the cocoa and hot water into a large mixing bowl and blend together until smooth. Add the remaining cake ingredients and beat well with an electric mixer until thoroughly blended.

3 Divide the mixture between the paper cases and bake in the preheated oven for about 20 minutes, or until well risen and the tops of the sponges spring back when lightly pressed with a finger.

4 Lift out and leave to cool on a wire rack.

5 To make the icing, measure the icing sugar into a bowl and add sufficient water to give a smooth coating consistency. Stir in the peppermint extract and food colouring and mix well. Spread a little of the icing on top of each cake and decorate with either a whole or half chocolate peppermint or a few chocolate mint balls, if using.

# APPLE AND MINCEMEAT SLICES

*I often make these at Christmas time, as they are less time-consuming than making individual pies. They're best eaten on the day they are made.*

**MAKES 24**
350g (12 oz) plain flour
175g (6 oz) butter
2 level tbsp icing sugar,
  plus extra to dust
2 large eggs

*For the filling*
75g (3 oz) demerara
  sugar
½ x 410g jar mincemeat
finely grated zest and
  juice of 1 lemon
1 level tsp ground
  mixed spice
2 large Bramley apples,
  peeled, cored and
  sliced

1 You will need a 33 x 23cm (13 x 9 in) Swiss roll tin.

2 Measure the flour and butter into a food processor and whizz until breadcrumb stage. Add the icing sugar and eggs and whizz until a dough is formed. Knead into a ball. Place just over a third of the pastry in the fridge and roll out the remaining pastry until thin. Use to line the tin, prick the base then leave in the fridge to chill for 30 minutes.

3 Preheat the oven to 200°C/Fan 180°C/Gas 6 and put a large baking sheet in the oven to get hot.

4 To make the filling, measure all the ingredients into a bowl and mix well.

5 Spread the filling over the top of the pastry in the tin. Grate the remaining chilled pastry over the top of the filling using a coarse grater and bake on the baking sheet in the preheated oven for about 30 minutes, until pale golden brown on top and underneath.

6 Dredge with a little icing sugar then leave to cool in the tin.

7 Cut into 24 fingers to serve.

# HONEY AND MINCEMEAT FINGERS

*These fingers are the perfect treat for people who think they don't like mincemeat
– they'll never know it's there! The mincemeat filling gives them a lovely flavour.
The baked mixture may also be cut into large pieces and served as a pudding.
If liked, the top may be covered with a little glacé icing.*

**MAKES 10**

100g (4 oz) self-raising
   flour
½ level tsp baking
   powder
75g (3 oz) butter,
   softened
50g (2 oz) caster sugar
75g (3 oz) quick
   porridge oats
3 level tbsp honey
½ x 410g jar mincemeat
demerara sugar,
   to sprinkle

1 Preheat the oven to 180°C/Fan 160°C/Gas 4 and grease a 17.5cm (7 in) square tin with butter.

2 Place all the ingredients except for the mincemeat and demerara sugar into a bowl and mix well with a wooden spoon to form a soft dough. Divide the mixture in two. Put one half of the mixture into the tin and press with a spoon to cover the base.

3 Spread the mincemeat over the top then dot with the remaining mixture. Gently spread the mixture out using a palette knife to completely cover the mincemeat. Sprinkle with demerara sugar.

4 Bake in the preheated oven for about 30–35 minutes, or until golden brown.

5 Leave to cool in the tin for 20 minutes then mark into 10 fingers. Serve when cold.

# CLASSIC SIMPLE MERINGUES

*Make meringues by this foolproof method and I guarantee success. Use non-stick silicone paper, which can be brushed off and used again and again. You can make these with light muscovado sugar, in which case they will be slightly darker when they are cooked than these very pale, off-white meringues.*

**MAKES 12 DOUBLE MERINGUES**

4 large egg whites
225g (8 oz) caster sugar
300ml (½ pint) double cream, whipped

1 Preheat the oven to 120°C/Fan 100°C/Gas ¼ and line two baking sheets with silicone paper.

2 Place the egg whites in a large bowl and whisk on high speed with an electric whisk until they form soft peaks.

3 Add the sugar, a generous dessertspoonful at a time, whisking well after each addition, until all the sugar has been added.

4 Using two dessertspoons, spoon the meringue out on to the baking sheets, putting 12 meringues on each tray.

5 Bake in the preheated oven for 3–4 hours, or until the meringues are firm and dry and will lift easily from the silicone paper. They will be a very pale off-white.

6 Whisk the cream until it is thick and use it to sandwich the meringues together.

# JUST ROCK CAKES

*Good old-fashioned rock cakes – quick and inexpensive to make. Eat on the day of baking as they are at their very best eaten fresh. They will freeze beautifully, too, so if you know that you are not going to eat them all at one sitting, freeze the remainder as soon as they are cool. If you like a spicier flavour, add ½ level teaspoon of mixed spice with the flour.*

**MAKES 12**
225g (8 oz) self-raising flour
100g (4 oz) baking spread, from fridge
50g (2 oz) granulated sugar
225g (8 oz) sultanas
1 large egg
about 1 tbsp milk
about 25g (1 oz) demerara sugar

**1** Preheat the oven to 200°C/Fan 180°C/Gas 6 and well grease two large baking sheets.

**2** Measure the flour into a large bowl and rub in the spread until the mixture resembles fine breadcrumbs. Add the sugar and fruit and toss together to mix. Add the egg and milk and blend to a really stiff mixture; if still too dry add a little more milk.

**3** Using two teaspoons, shape the mixture into 12 rough mounds on the baking sheets, sprinkle with the demerara sugar and bake in the preheated oven for about 15 minutes, until pale golden brown at the edges.

**4** Lift off with a palette knife and leave to cool on a wire rack.

# COCONUT MERINGUE SLICES

*These delicious fingers of sponge keep well. For a change, sprinkle the top with finely chopped glacé cherries.*

**MAKES 16**

75g (3 oz) baking spread, from fridge
100g (4 oz) caster sugar
2 large egg yolks
2 tbsp milk
a few drops vanilla extract
175g (6 oz) self-raising flour

**For the topping**
2 large egg whites
100g (4 oz) caster sugar
50g (2 oz) desiccated coconut
flaked almonds

1 Preheat the oven to 160°C/Fan 140°C/Gas 3 and line a 27.5 x 17.5cm (11 x 7 in) baking tin with non-stick baking paper.

2 Cream the spread and sugar together until soft. Beat in the egg yolks, milk and vanilla extract and lastly fold in the flour – the mixture will be quite stiff. Spread it carefully in a smooth layer over the base of the tin.

3 Place the egg whites in a large bowl and whisk with an electric whisk until stiff. Add in the sugar a generous dessertspoonful at a time. Fold in the desiccated coconut. Spread over the cake mixture and sprinkle with flaked almonds.

4 Bake in the preheated oven for about 35 minutes, by which time the meringue will be firm to the touch and a pale golden brown.

5 Leave to cool in the tin.

6 Cut into 16 slices to serve.

# CHEWY DATE BARS

*These are so good – ideal to pop into a lunch box. Store them in an airtight tin.*

**MAKES 16**

100g (4 oz) baking spread, from fridge
100g (4 oz) granulated sugar
2 large eggs
100g (4 oz) plain flour
1 tsp vanilla extract
100g (4 oz) semi-dried Medjool dates, stoned and finely chopped

1 Preheat the oven to 180°C/Fan 160°C/Gas 4. Grease and flour a 17.5cm (7 in) square tin.

2 Measure all the ingredients, except the dates, into a large bowl and beat with an electric mixer until well blended and smooth. Stir in the dates.

3 Turn the mixture into the tin and smooth flat. Bake in the preheated oven for 20–25 minutes, until a pale golden brown all over.

4 Leave to cool in the tin.

5 Cut into 16 bars to serve.

# ORANGE FRUIT CRUNCH FINGERS

*These are lovely in a lunch box or served warm, as a pudding, with ice cream.*

**MAKES 8**

finely grated zest and
   juice of 1 orange
50g (2 oz) semi-dried
   Medjool dates, stoned
   and chopped or cut
   with scissors
25g (1 oz) seedless
   raisins
100g (4 oz) quick
   porridge oats
40g (1½ oz) plain flour
40g (1½ oz) demerara
   sugar
75g (3 oz) butter

1 Preheat the oven to 190°C/Fan 170°C /Gas 5 and grease
a 17.5cm (7 in) square tin.

2 Make up the orange juice to 150ml (¼ pint) with water and
put in a small saucepan. Add the dates and raisins and cook
over a gentle heat until the mixture is thick – this will take
about 10 minutes. Turn out on to a flat plate, spread out
and leave to cool.

3 Meanwhile, measure the oats, flour and sugar into a large
bowl with the zest and rub in the butter. Press half this mixture
into the tin and cover with the cooled fruit. Sprinkle with the
remaining mixture, press down lightly and bake in the preheated
oven for about 40 minutes.

4 Leave to cool in the tin for 20 minutes, then mark into
8 fingers and leave to cool completely.

# BLUEBERRY MUFFINS

*These are quick, easy and perfect for breakfast or the lunch box.*

**MAKES 12**
2 large eggs
75g (3 oz) caster sugar
225ml (8 fl oz) milk
100g (4 oz) butter,
    melted and cooled
1 tsp vanilla extract
finely grated zest
    of 1 lemon
275g (10 oz) self-raising
    flour
1 level tsp baking
    powder
200g (7 oz) blueberries

**1** Preheat the oven to 200°C/Fan 180°C/Gas 6 and arrange 12 muffin cases in a muffin tin.

**2** Measure the eggs, sugar, milk, butter, vanilla and lemon zest into a large bowl and beat with an electric mixer. Sift in the flour and baking powder and beat again until just blended.

**3** Finally, fold in the blueberries then spoon into the cases. Bake in the preheated oven for 25–30 minutes, until well risen and lightly golden brown.

**4** Lift out and cool on a wire rack.

# MARMALADE SURPRISE CAKES

*If liked these small cakes can be iced with a little orange glacé icing.*

**MAKES 24**
225g (8 oz) plain flour
100g (4 oz) butter
about 8 tsp water
about 4 tbsp orange
  marmalade
icing sugar, to dust

*For the topping*
100g (4 oz) baking
  spread, from fridge
100g (4 oz) caster sugar
2 large eggs
100g (4 oz) self-raising
  flour
½ level tsp baking
  powder
finely grated zest
  of 1 orange

1 Preheat the oven to 180°C/Fan 160°C/Gas 4. You will need two 12-hole muffin tins.

2 Measure the flour into a bowl and rub in the butter until the mixture resembles fine breadcrumbs. Mix to a firm dough with the water. Knead until smooth then roll out on a lightly floured surface. Cut out 24 circles with a 8cm (3 in) fluted pastry cutter and use to line the muffin tins.

3 Place ½ teaspoonful of marmalade in each pastry case.

4 To make the topping, measure all the ingredients into a mixing bowl and beat with an electric mixer until well blended.

5 Spoon teaspoonfuls of the mixture on top of the marmalade to completely cover then bake in the preheated oven for about 35 minutes, until the topping is golden brown and the pastry is cooked underneath.

6 Leave to cool in the tins for a few moments then lift out carefully with a knife and finish cooling on a wire rack. Dust with icing sugar to serve.

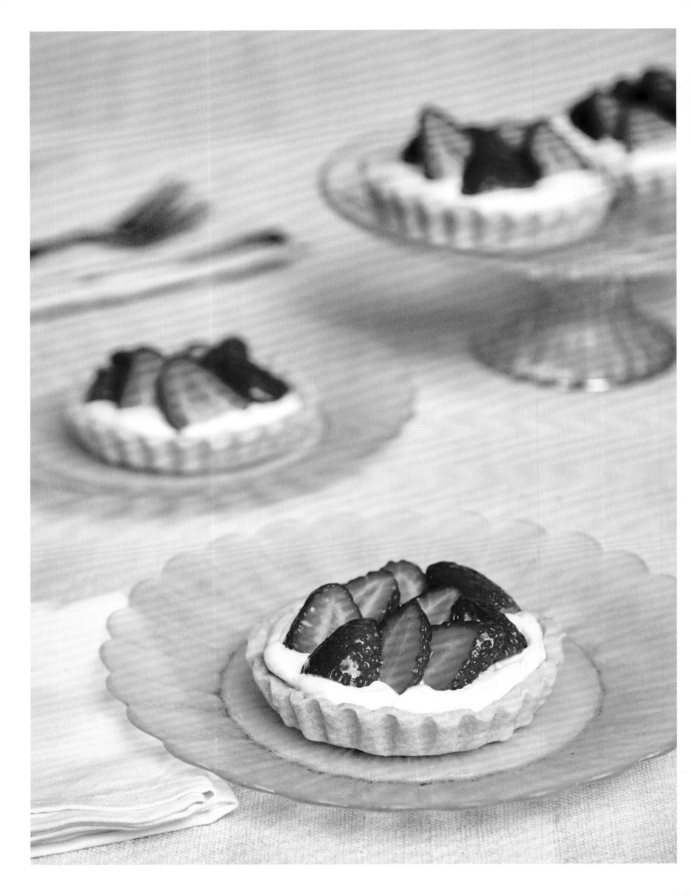

# STRAWBERRY CREAM TARTS

*If you have a glut of raspberries use them in place of strawberries. These little tarts are delicious to eat, sitting outside, at a special summer coffee party.*

**MAKES 6**

1 x 320g packet
  ready-rolled
  shortcrust pastry
200ml (7 fl oz) double
  cream
1 level tbsp icing sugar
½ tsp vanilla extract
350g (12 oz)
  strawberries, hulled
  and each cut into
  3 slices
3 tbsp redcurrant jelly

**1** You will need six 8cm (3 in) loose-bottomed fluted mini tart tins.

**2** Unroll the pastry on to a lightly floured surface and roll to a slightly thinner thickness. Stamp out 6 circles with a 12.5cm (5 in) round cutter and use to line the tins. Prick the bases and sides with a fork and leave to chill for about 30 minutes.

**3** Preheat the oven to 200°C/Fan 180°C/Gas 6.

**4** Line each tart with a small piece of baking paper, weigh down with baking beans and bake in the preheated oven for 10 minutes.

**5** Remove the paper and beans and bake for a further 5 minutes, until pale golden and crisp.

**6** Remove from the oven and leave to cool on a wire rack.

**7** Meanwhile, whisk the cream with the icing sugar and vanilla to soft peaks. Divide between the cooled pastry cases and arrange the strawberries on top.

**8** Melt the redcurrant jelly with 1 tablespoon of water in a small pan over a gentle heat, stirring until smooth, and then spoon or brush over the tarts. Leave to set.

# YORKSHIRE CAKES

*These are delicious small tarts with a spongy filling.*

**MAKES 24**
225g (8 oz) plain flour
100g (4 oz) butter
about 8 tsp water
about 4 tbsp raspberry
    jam

*For the topping*
100g (4 oz) baking
    spread, from fridge
225g (8 oz) caster sugar
2 large eggs
100g (4 oz) semolina
    or ground rice
50g (2 oz) currants

1 Preheat the oven to 200°C/Fan 180°C/Gas 6. You will need two 12-hole muffin tins.

2 Measure the flour into a bowl and rub in the butter until the mixture resembles fine breadcrumbs. Mix to a firm dough with the water. Knead until smooth then roll out on a lightly floured surface. Cut out 24 circles with a 8cm (3 in) cutter and use to line the muffin tins.

3 Spoon ½ teaspoon of jam into the bottom of each pastry case.

4 To make the topping, measure all the ingredients into a bowl and beat with an electric mixer until well blended.

5 Spoon teaspoonfuls of the mixture on top of the jam to cover then bake in the preheated oven for 20–25 minutes, until the topping is golden brown and the pastry is cooked underneath.

6 Leave to cool in the tins for a few moments then lift out carefully with a knife and finish cooling on a wire rack.

# QUICK BAKLAVA

*Serve this pastry warm with whipped cream. Filo pastry is readily available from good Greek shops, delicatessens and most supermarkets.*

**MAKES 16**
250g (9 oz) filo pastry
100g (4 oz) unsalted
  butter, melted
grated zest and juice
  of 1 lemon
100g (4 oz) walnuts,
  finely chopped
25g (1 oz) demerara
  sugar

**For the syrup**
150ml (¼ pint) water
225g (8 oz) caster sugar

**1** Preheat the oven to 200°C/Fan 180°C/Gas 6 and lightly butter a 27.5 x 17.5cm (11 x 7 in) baking tin.

**2** Cut the pastry sheets in half so that they are roughly the size of the tin. Lay 1 sheet of pastry in the tin, brush with melted butter and continue until there are 8 layers of pastry in the tin. Brush the top layer with melted butter and sprinkle with the lemon zest, nuts and sugar. Continue to add 8 more layers of pastry, brushing with butter between each layer. Finally, brush the top with more butter then cut the pastry with a very sharp knife into 16 equal-sized pieces.

**3** Bake in the preheated oven for about 30 minutes, until pale golden brown.

**4** Leave to cool in the tin.

**5** To make the syrup, measure the water and sugar into a pan and slowly bring it to the boil. Simmer for about 15 minutes without a lid to give a light syrup.

**6** Remove from the heat, stir in the juice of the lemon, and pour over the baklava.

# PALMIERS

*Best eaten when freshly made. These are good served with ice cream.*

**MAKES 24**

1 x 320g packet
   ready-rolled puff
   pastry
100g (4 oz) demerara
   sugar
1 level tsp ground
   cinnamon
a little milk, to glaze
1 large egg white,
   beaten with a fork

**1** Unroll the pastry and dust lightly with flour. Place non-stick paper over the top of the pastry and roll out to a slightly thinner rectangle measuring 33 x 27.5cm (13 x 11 in). Sprinkle one half of the pastry with half the demerara sugar and all of the cinnamon. Fold the pastry in half to cover the sugar. Reroll the pastry to a rectangle measuring 27.5 x 23 cm (11 x 9 in). Brush the surface with a little milk, then carefully roll both short sides into the centre of the pastry to make two tight rolls. Leave to chill in the fridge for 30 minutes.

**2** Preheat the oven to 220°C/Fan 200°C/Gas 7 and line two large baking sheets with non-stick baking paper.

**3** Slice the pastry into 1cm (½ in) slices to make 24 palmiers and place on the baking sheets. Brush with a little beaten egg white and sprinkle with half the remaining sugar. Bake in the preheated oven for 8 minutes.

**4** Remove the palmiers from the oven, turn them over and brush the tops with more beaten egg white. Sprinkle with the remaining demerara and return them to the oven for a further 8 minutes, until golden brown on both sides.

**5** Lift off with a palette knife and leave to cool on a wire rack.

# BISCUITS AND COOKIES

# PROPER SHORTBREAD

*Delicious with a cup of tea.*

**MAKES 24**
225g (8 oz) butter, softened
100g (4 oz) caster sugar
225g (8 oz) plain flour
100g (4 oz) semolina
2 level tbsp demerara sugar

1 Preheat the oven to 160°C/Fan 140°C/Gas 3. You will need a 30 x 23cm (12 x 9 in) traybake tin.

2 Cream the butter and sugar together in a mixing bowl. Work in the flour and semolina and bring together using your hands into a soft dough.

3 Press the mixture into the tin, level and smooth the top using the back of a spoon, and sprinkle with demerara sugar. Bake in the preheated oven for about 55 minutes, until a pale golden brown.

4 Remove from the oven, leave for 5 minutes, then mark into 24 triangles. Leave in the tin to become cold before lifting out on to a wire rack.

# LEMON SHORTBREAD

*This really is quite one of my favourite shortbreads. It keeps extremely well in an airtight tin and is delicious to serve with a cup of coffee.*

**MAKES 12**

100g (4 oz) butter, softened
50g (2 oz) caster sugar, plus extra to sprinkle
100g (4 oz) plain flour
50g (2 oz) cornflour
finely grated zest of 1 large lemon

1 Preheat the oven to 160°C/Fan 140°C/Gas 3. You will need a 17.5cm (7 in) square tin.

2 Cream the butter and sugar together in a bowl until light and fluffy. Work in the flours and lemon zest and knead well together.

3 Press the mixture into the tin, level and smooth the top using the back of a spoon. Bake in the preheated oven for about 50–55 minutes, until a pale golden brown.

4 Remove from the oven and mark into 12 fingers. Leave to cool in the tin then lift out on to a wire rack.

5 Sprinkle with caster sugar to serve.

# APRICOT SHORTBREAD

*Apricots are added to this basic shortbread to give it a nice flavour and texture.*
*This is a good recipe to prepare for a bazaar or for a bring-and-buy sale.*

**MAKES 12**
100g (4 oz) butter,
   softened
50g (2 oz) caster sugar
100g (4 oz) plain flour
50g (2 oz) cornflour
25g (1 oz) ready-to-
   eat dried apricots,
   finely chopped
icing sugar, sifted

1 Preheat the oven to 160°C/Fan 140°C/Gas 3. You will need a 17.5cm (7 in) square tin.

2 Cream the butter and sugar together in a bowl until light and fluffy. Work in the flours and the apricots and knead well together.

3 Press the mixture into the tin, level and smooth the top using the back of a spoon. Bake in the preheated oven for about 50–55 minutes, until a very pale golden brown.

4 Remove from the oven and mark into 12 fingers. Leave to cool in the tin then lift out on to a wire rack.

5 Sprinkle with icing sugar to serve.

# VIENNESE FINGER BISCUITS

*This is a basic recipe that can be adapted very easily to make all sorts of interesting biscuits.*

**MAKES 25–30**

225g (8 oz) butter,
    very softened
50g (2 oz) icing sugar
225g (8 oz) plain flour
1 tsp vanilla extract

1 Preheat the oven to 160°C/Fan 140°C/Gas 3 and line two baking sheets with non-stick baking paper.

2 Put the ingredients into a food processor and whizz until you have a smooth, soft dough.

3 Place the mixture in a piping bag fitted with a large star nozzle and pipe out into 5–7.5cm (2–3 in) lengths. If time allows, leave to chill in the fridge for 30 minutes, until very firm.

4 Bake the biscuits in the preheated oven for about 40 minutes, until light, pale golden brown at the edges.

5 Leave to cool on the sheets for a few moments then lift off with a palette knife and finish cooling on a wire rack.

---

**VARIATION: CHOCOLATE FINGERS**

Make and pipe as in the basic recipe. When cold, dip the ends of the biscuits in a little melted chocolate and leave to set.

# TRADITIONAL DUTCH BUTTER BISCUITS

*These biscuits really should be made with butter as the flavour of margarine doesn't do them justice.*

**MAKES ABOUT 20**
225g (8 oz) unsalted
    butter, softened
100g (4 oz) caster sugar
1 large egg yolk
200g (7 oz) plain flour
75g (3 oz) ground
    almonds
a little icing sugar,
    to dust

1 Line two or three large baking sheets with non-stick baking paper.

2 Measure all the ingredients except the icing sugar into a large mixing bowl and work together until thoroughly mixed and smooth (this can be done most quickly in a processor or food mixer).

3 Place the mixture in a piping bag fitted with a large rose nozzle and pipe the mixture into rounds on the prepared baking sheets. Leave to chill in the fridge for 30 minutes, until firm.

4 Preheat the oven to 190°C/Fan 170°C/Gas 5.

5 Bake in the preheated oven for about 10 minutes until just beginning to colour at the edges.

6 Leave to cool on the sheets for a few moments then lift off with a palette knife and finish cooling on a wire rack.

7 Serve dusted with a little icing sugar.

# CINNAMON CRISPY BISCUITS

*Lovely crunchy biscuits, always popular in our biscuit tin.*

**MAKES ABOUT 36**

225g (8 oz) butter, softened
225g (8 oz) demerara sugar
225g (8 oz) self-raising flour
½ level tsp ground mixed spice
2 level tsp ground cinnamon
1 large egg, beaten

**1** Heat the oven to 200°C/Fan 180°C /Gas 6 and line three large baking sheets with non-stick baking paper, or bake in batches.

**2** Measure all the ingredients into a mixing bowl and beat with an electric mixer until well blended and smooth.

**3** Roll the mixture into small balls and place on to the baking sheets. Press down slightly to flatten the balls and bake in the preheated oven for about 12 minutes, until golden brown.

**4** Leave to cool on the sheets for a few moments then lift off with a palette knife and finish cooling on a wire rack.

# DANISH LACE BISCUITS

*These are very thin almondy biscuits, which are good to serve with cold desserts.*

**MAKES ABOUT 24**
50g (2 oz) blanched
    almonds, chopped
75g (3 oz) plain flour
75g (3 oz) caster sugar
75g (3 oz) butter,
    softened

**1** Preheat the oven to 180°C/Fan 160°C/Gas 4 and line four large baking sheets with non-stick baking paper, or bake in batches using two large baking sheets.

**2** Measure all the ingredients into a bowl and work together with a wooden spoon to form a firm dough. Knead gently until smooth.

**3** Take teaspoonfuls of the mixture, roll into balls and arrange on the baking sheets, leaving plenty of room for them to spread. Press down with a fork to flatten them then reshape to a circle with the back of the fork.

**4** Bake in the preheated oven for about 12 minutes, until just beginning to turn golden brown at the edges.

**5** Leave to cool on the sheets for a moment then lift off with a palette knife on to a wire rack to finish cooling.

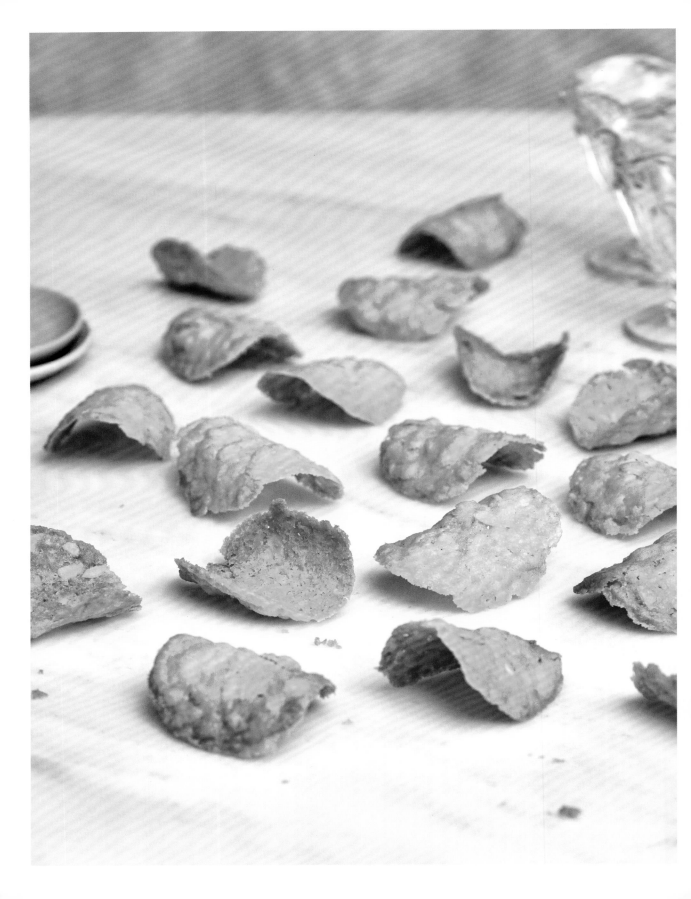

# ALMOND CRISPS

*These biscuits are perfect to serve with mousses and fools. They seem to lose their flavour quite quickly in a tin so they are best served fresh.*

**MAKES ABOUT 18**

65g (2½ oz) butter, softened
50g (2 oz) caster sugar
40g (1½ oz) plain flour
40g (1½ oz) flaked almonds

1 Preheat the oven to 180°C/Fan 160°C/Gas 4 and line a baking sheet with non-stick baking paper. You will need a couple of lightly oiled rolling pins.

2 Cream the butter and sugar until very pale then stir in the flour and almonds. Shape the mixture into marble-sized balls and place them about 7.5cm (3 in) apart on the baking sheet. Only bake one sheet at a time (you will need to work fast once they are baked).

3 Flatten the balls with a damp fork and bake in the preheated oven for 8–10 minutes, until a pale golden brown.

4 Remove the biscuits from the oven, leave to cool for 30–60 seconds then lift off each one very carefully with a palette knife and lay over a lightly oiled rolling pin and leave to harden. They are very fragile so be light fingered!

5 When they have hardened, lift off very carefully and store in an airtight container.

# OLD ENGLISH JUMBLES

*Jumbles are traditionally made in the shape of an 'S'. However, if time is short, you may find it quicker to roll the mixture out into small balls. Press them flat with two fingers before baking. These biscuits keep well if stored in an airtight tin.*

**MAKES ABOUT 20**
65g (2½ oz) butter,
　　softened
65g (2½ oz) caster sugar
1 large egg yolk
finely grated zest
　　of 1 lemon
25g (1 oz) ground
　　almonds
150g (5 oz) plain flour
½ level tsp ground
　　mixed spice
1 tbsp milk

1 Preheat the oven to 180°C/Fan 160°C/Gas 4 and line two baking sheets with non-stick baking paper.

2 Cream the butter with the sugar until light and fluffy. Beat in the egg yolk and all the remaining ingredients. If the dough is too stiff and crumbly to roll, add another tablespoon of milk.

3 Take small pieces of the dough, roll each out into a strip and then form into an 'S' and lay it on the baking sheet. Repeat with the remaining dough. Bake in the preheated oven for about 15–20 minutes, until tinged a pale golden brown at the edges.

4 Lift off with a palette knife and leave to cool on a wire rack.

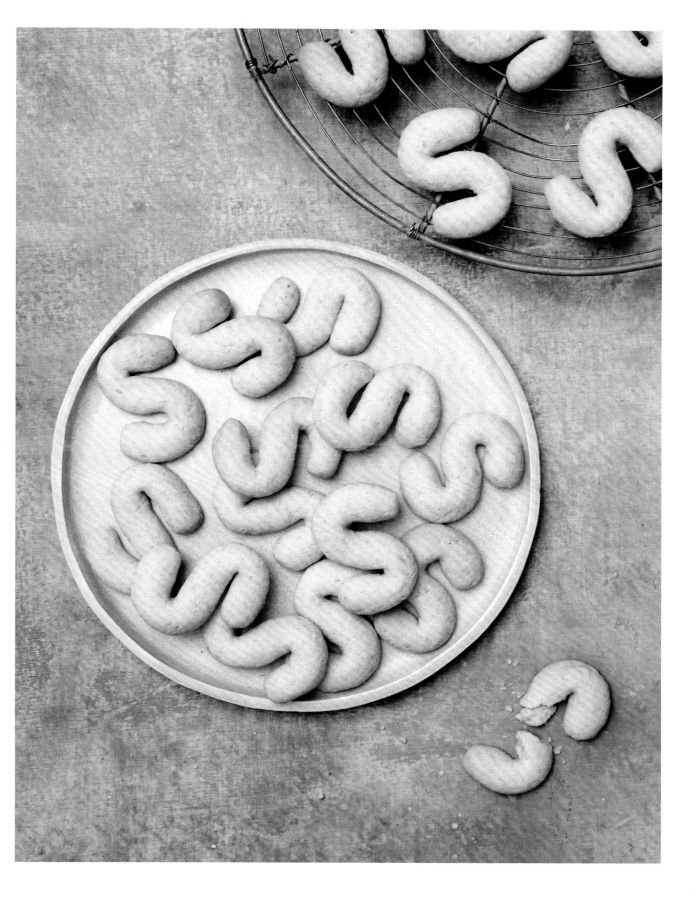

# HURDON FARMHOUSE BISCUITS

*These biscuits are a bit fiddly to prepare but it's worth persevering as the end result looks good and tastes delicious.*

**MAKES ABOUT 50**
350g (12 oz) self-raising
    flour
225g (8 oz) butter
175g (6 oz) caster sugar
1 large egg, beaten
25g (1 oz) porridge oats,
    to coat

1 Preheat the oven to 180°C/160°C/Gas 4 and line two or three large baking sheets with non-stick baking paper, or bake in batches.

2 Measure the flour into a large mixing bowl and rub in the butter until the mixture resembles fine breadcrumbs. Stir in the sugar and bind to a dough with the beaten egg. Knead until smooth.

3 Take teaspoonfuls of the mixture and roll them into balls. Press the balls down into the porridge oats to flatten them into rounds and coat lightly with the oats. Arrange on the baking sheets and bake in the preheated oven for about 15–20 minutes, until pale golden brown.

4 Leave to cool on the sheets for a few moments then lift off with a palette knife and finish cooling on a wire rack.

# MUESLI JACKS

*These biscuits are a good way of turning unwanted breakfast cereal into a family favourite. You can use any cereal but we like adding one with fruit and nuts. If the cereal is particularly sweet, you could reduce the amount of demerara sugar.*

**MAKES ABOUT 24**
100g (4 oz) butter
1 rounded tbsp golden
  syrup
100g (4 oz) demerara
  sugar
75g (3 oz) mixed cereal
  with fruit and nuts
75g (3 oz) self-raising
  flour

1 Preheat the oven to 160°C/Fan 140°C/Gas 3 and line three large baking sheets with non-stick baking paper, or bake in batches.

2 Measure the butter, syrup and sugar into a saucepan and place over a gentle heat until the butter has melted.

3 Remove from the heat and measure in the mixed cereal and flour. Stir well.

4 Allow the mixture to cool slightly then roll into small balls and place them, well spaced, on the baking sheets. Bake in the preheated oven for about 15–20 minutes, until a pale golden brown all over.

5 Leave to cool on the sheets for a few moments then lift off with a palette knife and finish cooling on a wire rack.

6 Store in an airtight tin.

# CHERRY AND NUT CRISPS

*These small flapjack-type biscuits keep very well and have an excellent flavour.*

**MAKES ABOUT 30**
100g (4 oz) demerara
   sugar
100g (4 oz) butter
100g (4 oz) golden syrup
100g (4 oz) plain flour
75g (3 oz) rolled oats
25g (1 oz) ground
   almonds
40g (1½ oz) blanched
   almonds, chopped
50g (2 oz) glacé cherries,
   chopped

**1** Preheat the oven to 180°C/Fan 160°C/Gas 4 and line two or three large baking sheets with non-stick baking paper, or bake in batches.

**2** Measure the sugar, butter and syrup into a saucepan and heat gently until the sugar has dissolved.

**3** Remove from the heat, add all the remaining ingredients and mix very thoroughly. Leave to cool.

**4** Roll the mixture into small balls, each about the size of a walnut, and place on the baking sheets. Flatten down slightly, allowing room for them to spread slightly and bake in the preheated oven for about 15 minutes, until a pale golden brown.

**5** Leave to cool on the sheets for a few moments then lift off with a palette knife and finish cooling on a wire rack.

**6** Store in an airtight tin.

# ABBEY BISCUITS

*Delicious – always a favourite oaty biscuit with a cup of coffee.*

**MAKES ABOUT 40**
150g (5 oz) plain flour
150g (5 oz) butter, softened
150g (5 oz) caster sugar
100g (4 oz) porridge oats
1 tbsp milk
1 rounded tbsp golden syrup
1 level tsp bicarbonate of soda

1 Preheat the oven to 160°C/Fan 140°C/Gas 3 and line four large baking sheets with non-stick baking paper, or bake in batches.

2 Measure all the ingredients into a bowl and work together until thoroughly blended.

3 Take teaspoonfuls of the mixture, roll into balls and arrange on the prepared baking sheets, leaving room for them to spread. Bake in the preheated oven for about 20 minutes, until golden brown.

4 Leave to cool on the sheets for a few moments then lift off with a palette knife and finish cooling on a wire rack.

# FAIRINGS

*A crisp biscuit with a mild ginger flavour.*

**MAKES 24**
175g (6 oz) self-raising
  flour
1½ level tsp ground
  ginger
pinch of bicarbonate
  of soda
75g (3 oz) caster sugar
75g (3 oz) butter
1 tbsp golden syrup

**1** Preheat the oven to 180°C/Fan 160°C/Gas 4 and line three large baking sheets with non-stick baking paper, or bake in batches.

**2** Sift the flour, ginger and bicarb together into a bowl.

**3** Measure the sugar, butter and syrup into a saucepan and heat gently until the butter has melted.

**4** Stir the melted mixture into the dry ingredients and mix to a stiff dough.

**5** Shape into 24 small balls or place in teaspoonfuls on the baking sheets and bake in the preheated oven for about 15 minutes, until golden brown at the edges.

**6** Leave to cool slightly then lift off with a palette knife and finish cooling on a wire rack.

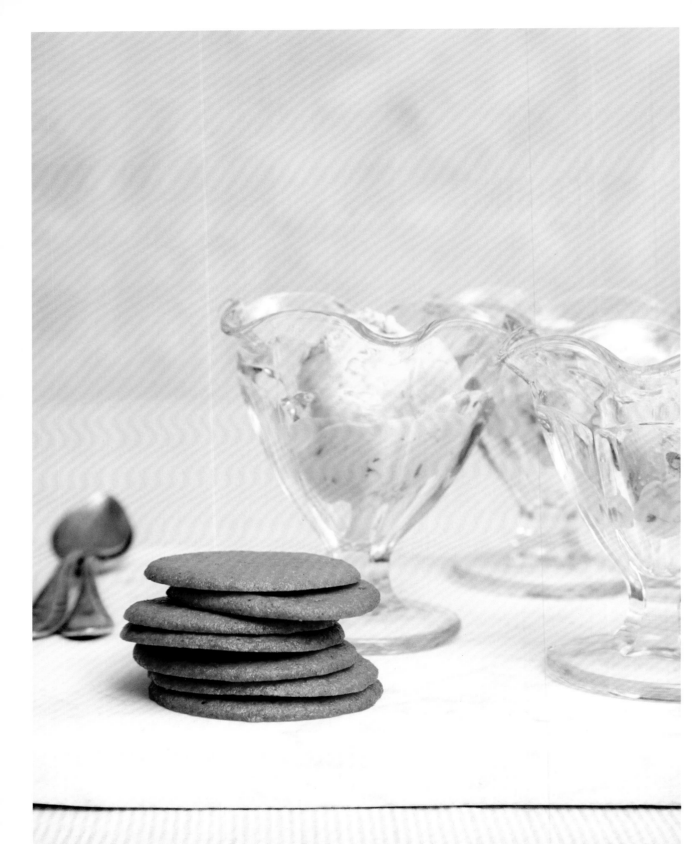

# SPICED BISCUIT THINS

*A special ginger biscuit that is good to serve with ice creams and sorbets.*

**MAKES 28**
100g (4 oz) golden syrup
50g (2 oz) butter
25g (1 oz) demerara
  sugar
100g (4 oz) plain flour
½ level tsp bicarbonate
  of soda
1½ level tsp ground
  ginger
½ level tsp ground
  mixed spice

1 Preheat the oven to 180°C/Fan 160°C/Gas 4 and line two large baking sheets with non-stick baking paper.

2 Measure the syrup, butter and sugar into a pan and place over a gentle heat until the butter has melted.

3 Measure the remaining ingredients into a bowl, add the melted mixture and beat well until thoroughly blended. Leave to cool to room temperature.

4 Spoon teaspoonfuls of the mixture on to the baking sheets, leaving room for them to spread. Bake in the preheated oven for 10–15 minutes, until dark golden brown.

5 Leave to cool slightly then lift off with a palette knife and finish cooling on a wire rack.

# GINGER COOKIES

*These can easily be fitted in with the rest of your plans for the day. The mixture can be prepared and left to chill whilst you are out shopping, then baked when you get back.*

**MAKES 36–40**
175g (6 oz) butter
125g (4½ oz) light
　muscovado sugar
2 level tsp ground
　ginger
225g (8 oz) plain flour
demerara sugar, to coat

1 Measure the butter and sugar into a bowl. Beat with an electric hand-held whisk until light and fluffy. Add the ginger and flour and beat into a soft dough.

2 Turn the dough out on to a lightly floured surface and knead until smooth. Roll into two sausage shapes about 18cm (7 in) long and 5cm (2 in) wide. Place each one on to a sheet of cling film and sprinkle generously with demerara sugar. Roll each sausage in the sugar until the surface is completely coated and the sugar is stuck to the dough. Wrap in the cling film and leave to chill in the fridge for about 30 minutes, until very firm.

3 Preheat the oven to 180°C/Fan 160°C/Gas 4 and line two large baking sheets with non-stick baking paper.

4 Cut each roll into about 18–20 slices and arrange, well-spaced, on the prepared baking sheets. Bake in the preheated oven for about 15 minutes, until pale golden brown at the edges.

5 Leave to cool on the sheets for a few moments then lift off with a palette knife and finish cooling on a wire rack.

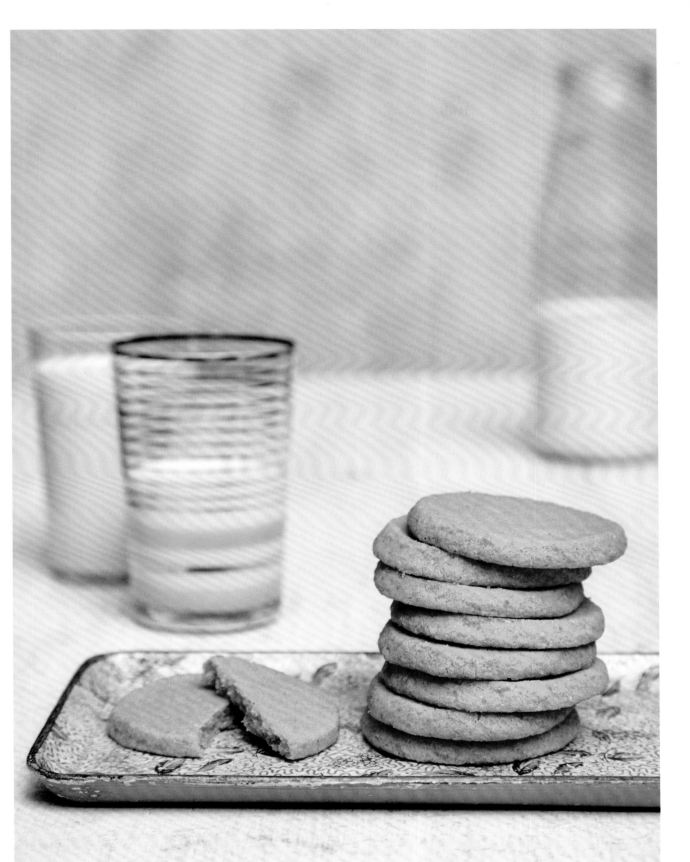

# GINGER AND CHOCOLATE CHIP SNAPS

*These ginger biscuits are quick to make as there is no stamping out of rounds –*
*just cutting slices from the roll.*

**MAKES 24**

225g (8 oz) plain flour
1 level tsp ground
   ginger
¼ level tsp bicarbonate
   of soda
70g (2½ oz) butter
75g (3 oz) golden syrup
100g (4 oz) chocolate
   chips

**1** Sift the flour, ginger and bicarb into a bowl and rub in the butter until the mixture resembles breadcrumbs. Add the golden syrup and chocolate chips and mix to a stiff dough – it is easier to use your hands.

**2** Roll the dough into a sausage about 24cm (9½ in) in length, wrap in cling film and leave to chill in the fridge for about 30 minutes, until firm.

**3** Preheat the oven to 200°C/Fan 180°C/Gas 4 and line two large baking sheets with non-stick baking paper.

**4** Cut the roll into about 24 thin slices and arrange on the baking sheets. Bake in the preheated oven for about 15 minutes, until a pale ginger colour.

**5** Lift off with a palette knife and leave to cool on a wire rack.

# BOTERMOPPEN

*These are Dutch shortbread biscuits and have a lovely flavour.*

**MAKES 32**

175g (6 oz) unsalted
   butter
finely grated zest of
   ½ lemon
100g (4 oz) caster sugar
225g (8 oz) plain flour
25g (1 oz) granulated
   sugar

**1** Cream the butter and lemon zest in a large bowl until soft, then beat in the sugar until the mixture is light. Blend in the flour and knead lightly until smooth (use your hands for this).

**2** Divide the mixture in two and roll out to form two 15cm (6 inch) sausages. Cover these in granulated sugar, wrap in cling film and leave to chill in the fridge for about 30 minutes, until firm.

**3** Preheat the oven to 160°C/Fan 140°C/Gas 3 and line two or three large baking sheets with non-stick baking paper, or bake in batches.

**4** Cut each sausage into 16 slices and place on the baking sheets, allowing a little room for them to spread. Bake in the preheated oven for about 25 minutes, until pale golden brown at the edges.

**5** Remove from the oven and carefully lift off with a palette knife to cool on a wire rack.

# SULTANA WALNUT COOKIES

*The sultanas and walnuts in these cookies combine well to give a very good flavour.*

**MAKES ABOUT 36**
100g (4 oz) butter,
    softened
100g (4 oz) light
    muscovado sugar
1 large egg, beaten
½ level tsp bicarbonate
    of soda
225g (8 oz) plain flour
100g (4 oz) sultanas
50g (2 oz) walnuts,
    chopped
finely grated zest
    of 1 orange

1 Preheat the oven to 180°C/Fan 160°C/Gas 4 and line two baking sheets with non-stick baking paper.

2 Measure the butter and sugar into a bowl and beat well until soft and creamy. Work in all the remaining ingredients until the mixture forms a stiff dough.

3 Divide the mixture into small pieces. Roll them into balls and place on the baking sheets. Press each one flat with a fork. Bake in the preheated oven for about 10–12 minutes, until a pale golden brown.

4 Lift off with a palette knife and leave to cool on a wire rack.

5 Store in an airtight tin.

# EASTER BISCUITS

*Be sure to use butter for these biscuits as the flavour really does come through.*

**MAKES ABOUT 24**

175g (6 oz) butter, softened
100g (4 oz) caster sugar, plus extra to glaze
finely grated zest of 1 lemon
2 large egg yolks, plus a little egg white, beaten, to glaze
225g (8 oz) plain flour
50g (2 oz) currants

1 Cream the butter with the sugar and lemon zest until light and fluffy. Work in the egg yolks then stir in the flour and currants. Knead lightly until smooth. Leave in the fridge to chill for about 1 hour, until firm.

2 Preheat the oven to 180°C/Fan 160°C/Gas 4 and line two baking sheets with non-stick baking paper.

3 Roll out the dough on a lightly floured surface to a 3mm (⅛ in) thickness and cut into rounds with a fluted 7.5cm (3 in) cutter.

4 Lift on to the baking sheets, brush with a little lightly beaten egg white and dredge with caster sugar. Bake in the preheated oven for 12–15 minutes, until just golden brown.

5 Lift off with a palette knife and leave to cool on a wire rack.

6 Store in an airtight tin.

# MEGA PEANUT BUTTER COOKIES

*These are great to keep in the biscuit tin as they are popular with children.*
*They are easy, too, as they are made with store-cupboard ingredients.*

**MAKES 24**
225g (8 oz) self-raising
    flour
150g (5 oz) butter,
    softened
50g (2 oz) crunchy
    peanut butter
150g (5 oz) light
    muscovado sugar
1 large egg, beaten

**1** Preheat the oven to 180°C/Fan 160°C/Gas 4 and line two large baking sheets with non-stick baking paper.

**2** Measure the flour into a bowl and add the butter, peanut butter and sugar. Rub the mixture with your fingertips until it is starting to come together. Add the egg and bring together to form a soft dough.

**3** Divide the mixture into 24 pieces, roll them into balls and place, well spaced, on the baking sheets. Press the balls flat with a damp fork. Bake in the preheated oven for about 12–15 minutes, until a pale golden brown.

**4** Leave on the baking sheet to harden for a few minutes then lift off with a palette knife on to a wire rack to cool.

**5** Store in an airtight tin.

# ENGLISH MACAROONS

*Rice paper is not always easy to buy so you could use non-stick silicone paper instead. Silicone paper is ideal for biscuits with a high sugar content and can be reused many times.*

**MAKES 16**
2 large eggs whites
125g (5 oz) ground
   almonds
175g (6 oz) caster sugar
8 blanched almonds,
   halved

**1** Preheat the oven to 150°C/Fan 130°C/Gas 2 and line two baking sheets with rice paper or non-stick silicone paper.

**2** Set about 1 teaspoonful of the egg white to one side in a small bowl then whisk the remaining egg whites with an electric whisk until they form soft peaks. Fold in the ground almonds and sugar.

**3** Place heaped teaspoonfuls of the mixture, well spaced, on the two baking sheets and smooth them out with the back of a spoon to form circles. Place a halved blanched almond in the centre of each one. Finally, brush the almonds and tops of the macaroons with a little of the reserved egg white and bake in the preheated oven for about 25 minutes, or until the macaroons are a pale, golden brown.

**4** Remove from the oven and leave to cool slightly before lifting from the baking sheets with a palette knife. If rice paper has been used, remove any excess paper from around the edges. Leave to cool completely before serving.

# FLORENTINES

*I usually have to make double the quantity of these very special biscuits –
they disappear so quickly.*

**MAKES 20**
50g (2 oz) butter
50g (2 oz) demerara
 sugar
50g (2 oz) golden syrup
50g (2 oz) plain flour
4 glacé cherries, finely
 chopped
50g (2 oz) currants
50g (2 oz) chopped nuts
 (such as almonds
 and walnuts)

*For the topping*
175g (6 oz) Bournville
 chocolate, melted

1 Preheat the oven to 180°C/Fan 160°C/Gas 4 and line three large
baking sheets with non-stick baking paper or silicone sheets,
or bake in batches.

2 Measure the butter, sugar and golden syrup into a small pan
and heat gently until the butter has melted.

3 Measure the flour, cherries, currants and nuts into a mixing bowl,
pour over the melted mixture and stir well until thoroughly mixed.

4 Spoon teaspoonfuls of the mixture on to the prepared baking
sheets, leaving plenty of space for them to spread, and bake in
the preheated oven for 8–10 minutes, until golden brown.

5 Allow to cool for a few moments then carefully lift off with
a palette knife and finish cooling on a wire rack. Watch that
the Florentines don't become too cool before moving, or they
will be difficult to lift off the sheet. If this does happen, put them
back in the oven for a minute so they warm through. They will
then lift off more easily.

6 When cold, spread a little melted chocolate over the flat base
of each Florentine. Mark a zigzag in the chocolate with a fork
and leave to set, chocolate side up, on the wire rack.

7 Store in an airtight tin.

# BRANDY SNAPS

*The quantities given here result in a lot of brandy snaps but they keep very well in an airtight tin. If only a few are required it is easy to make half the quantity. They may be served just as they are with ice cream, mousses or soufflés but are also good if you fill them with a little whipped cream and serve them with fruit.*

**MAKES 30**

100g (4 oz) butter
100g (4 oz) demerara
   sugar
100g (4 oz) golden syrup
100g (4 oz) plain flour
1 level tsp ground
   ginger
1 tsp lemon juice

1 Preheat the oven to 180°C/Fan 160°C/Gas 4, line two or three large baking sheets with non-stick baking paper and oil the handles of four wooden spoons.

2 Measure the butter, sugar and syrup into a heavy-based saucepan and heat gently until the butter and sugar have dissolved – this will take about 15 minutes. Allow the mixture to cool slightly, about 2–3 minutes, then sift in the flour and ginger. Stir well, adding the lemon juice. Leave to cool to room temperature.

3 Place teaspoonfuls of the mixture on to the baking sheets, at least 10cm (4 in) apart. It is best to put only four spoonfuls on a baking sheet at any one time and to bake only one sheet at a time (you will need to work fast once they are baked). Bake in the preheated oven for about 10–15 minutes until golden brown.

4 Remove from the oven and leave for a few minutes to firm, then lift from the sheet with a palette knife. Immediately roll around the wooden spoons and leave to set on a wire rack with the join underneath. Then slip out the spoons. Watch that they don't become too cool before moving, or they will be difficult to lift off the sheet. If this does happen, put them back in the oven for a minute so they warm through. They will then lift off more easily.

5 Store in an airtight tin as soon as they are cold; they will keep for at least a week.

# LANCASHIRE BISCUITS

*Cheese is always very popular served after a meal, particularly with the male members of the family. I like to have a few of these biscuits stored away in an airtight tin to serve with a selection of cheese.*

**MAKES ABOUT 20**

100g (4 oz) baking spread
50g (2 oz) semolina
100g (4 oz) self-raising flour
75g (3 oz) mature Lancashire cheese, finely grated
½ level tsp salt
½ level tsp mustard powder
a generous pinch of cayenne pepper

1 Measure all the ingredients into a large mixing bowl and beat with an electric mixer until well blended and smooth. Knead well then roll into a sausage shape about 15cm (6 in) long. Wrap in cling film and leave to chill in the fridge for about 30 minutes, until firm.

2 Preheat the oven to 180°C/Fan 160°C/Gas 4 and line two baking sheets with non-stick baking paper.

3 Cut the roll into about 20 slices and arrange on the baking sheets. Bake in the preheated oven for about 20 minutes, until golden brown.

4 Leave to cool on the sheets for a few moments then lift off with a palette knife and finish cooling on a wire rack.

CHAPTER SEVEN

# ESPECIALLY FOR CHILDREN

# JELLY TOT CAKES

*These tiny cakes are made in petits four paper cases. They are so small that children can eat several at a time and seem to enjoy the novelty of them more than a large fairy cake or bun. My grandchildren enjoy helping to make these, particularly putting the sweets on top.*

**MAKES ABOUT 24**

75g (3 oz) baking spread, from fridge
2 large eggs
100g (4 oz) self-raising flour
½ level tsp baking powder
75g (3 oz) caster sugar
1 tbsp milk

*For the icing*
100g (4 oz) icing sugar, sifted
about 1 tbsp lemon juice

*For the decoration*
about 24 Jelly Tots

**1** Preheat the oven to 180°C/Fan 160°C/Gas 4 and arrange about 24 petits four cases on a large baking sheet or in mini muffin tins.

**2** Measure all the cake ingredients into a bowl and beat well with an electric mixer until thoroughly blended.

**3** Spoon teaspoonfuls of the mixture into the cases until they are almost three-quarters full. Be careful not to overfill the cases as the mixture will rise during baking. Bake in the preheated oven for about 15–20 minutes, until well risen and pale golden brown.

**4** Lift off and cool on wire racks.

**5** Measure the icing sugar into a bowl and add sufficient lemon juice to give a spreading consistency. Spoon a little on top of each cake and spread out with the back of a teaspoon. When the icing has almost set, top with a Jelly Tot.

# ICED SHAPE BISCUITS

*My grandchildren adore these. You could use any shapes – stars work well as decorations for the Christmas tree but you could make rabbits for Easter or any other shapes for a children's party. Let your children be creative – colour the icing if wished and have fun with them!*

**MAKES ABOUT 36**
100g (4 oz) butter,
    softened
100g (4 oz) caster sugar
200g (7 oz) plain flour
25g (1 oz) semolina
finely grated zest of
    1 lemon
1 large egg, beaten

**To decorate**
225g (8 oz) icing sugar,
    sifted
food colouring
    (optional)

1 Preheat the oven to 190°C/Fan 170°C/Gas 5 and lightly grease two or three large baking sheets.

2 Measure all the ingredients into a large mixing bowl and beat with an electric mixer until well blended. Turn out on to a lightly floured surface and knead until smooth.

3 Roll out to a 3mm (⅛ in) thickness, then use your preferred cutter to cut out different shapes. Lift the biscuits on to the baking sheets with a palette knife, re-roll and cut out the trimmings until all the dough has been used.

4 Bake in the preheated oven for about 10 minutes, until just beginning to tinge with golden brown.

5 Lift off with a palette knife and leave to cool on a wire rack.

6 Measure the icing sugar into a bowl and work in enough water to give a smooth glacé icing, adding colouring as wished. Spread some icing on the top of each biscuit to decorate.

# AFGHANS

*Everybody's favourites; children love making and eating these.*

**MAKES 30–35**
175g (6 oz) butter,
   softened
100g (4 oz) caster sugar
150g (5 oz) plain flour
2 level tbsp cocoa
   powder
50g (2 oz) crushed
   cornflakes

1 Preheat the oven to 180°C/Fan 160°C/Gas 4 and grease two or three large baking sheets, or bake in batches.

2 Cream the butter and sugar together until soft then gradually work in the flour, cocoa and, lastly, the crushed cornflakes.

3 Shape the mixture into small balls the size of a walnut and place, well spaced, on the baking sheets. Press each ball down with two fingers. Bake in the preheated oven for 15–20 minutes.

4 Lift off with a palette knife and leave to cool on a wire rack. Store in an airtight tin.

# CRUNCHIES

*Children adore these crunchies, and it's nice to include a couple in a packed lunch.*

**MAKES 20**

100g (4 oz) baking spread, from fridge
75g (3 oz) caster sugar
1 large egg yolk
150g (5 oz) self-raising flour
about 25g (1 oz) Rice Krispies

1 Heat the oven to 180°C/Fan 160°C/Gas 4 and line two large baking sheets with non-stick baking paper.

2 Measure all the ingredients except the Rice Krispies into a mixing bowl and work together using a wooden spoon until well mixed and smooth.

3 Take heaped teaspoonfuls of the mixture and roll into 20 balls. Roll each one in the Rice Krispies and arrange well spaced on the baking sheets. Slightly flatten each one and bake in the preheated oven for about 25 minutes, until just beginning to colour at the edges.

4 Leave to cool on the sheets for a few moments then lift off with a palette knife and finish cooling on a wire rack.

# TRAFFIC LIGHTS

*These are very easy to make and are ideal for a children's party.*

**MAKES 8**

175g (6 oz) Bournville chocolate

75g (3 oz) broken biscuits, roughly crushed

½ x 397g can full-fat condensed milk

red, yellow and green glacé cherries, halved

**1** Grease a 17.5cm (7 in) square cake tin and line with non-stick baking paper.

**2** Break the chocolate into small pieces and melt in a heatproof bowl over a pan of hot water. Stir occasionally until quite smooth.

**3** Remove from the heat and stir in the biscuits and condensed milk. Turn into the tin and smooth flat with the back of a spoon.

**4** Leave to chill in the fridge for about 6 hours, until set.

**5** Cut into 8 bars and decorate with the halved cherries in a traffic light pattern.

# CAROLINE'S CHOCOLATE SLAB

*This is very popular with all my family and is an ideal recipe for children to make on their own. Any plain biscuits will do for this; it is a good way of using up the broken pieces from the bottom of the biscuit tin.*

MAKES 16

175g (6 oz) plain
   digestive biscuits
100g (4 oz) caster sugar
100g (4 oz) butter
100g (4 oz) Bournville
   chocolate
50g (2 oz) sultanas

1 Line a 17.5cm (7 in) square cake tin with cling film.

2 Put the biscuits in a plastic bag and crush with a rolling pin into small pieces.

3 Measure the sugar and butter into a pan and heat gently until the butter has melted.

4 Remove the pan from the heat and stir in the chocolate until melted. Add the crushed biscuits and sultanas and mix well.

5 Press the mixture into the tin and smooth the top. Leave to chill in the fridge for about 6 hours, until set.

6 Cut into 16 squares and store in an airtight tin.

# PEANUT SQUARES

*These are easy to make and could be made by children. Use any broken biscuits that have accumulated at the bottom of the biscuit tin.*

**MAKES 16**
75g (3 oz) butter
50g (2 oz) light
   muscovado sugar
4 tbsp golden syrup
4 tbsp crunchy peanut
   butter
175g (6 oz) broken
   biscuits, lightly
   crushed

1 Wet a 17.5cm (7 in) square cake tin with water, then line with a piece of cling film.

2 Place the butter in a small pan with the sugar and golden syrup and bring slowly to the boil, stirring until the sugar has dissolved and the butter has melted.

3 Remove from the heat and stir in the peanut butter. Finally, add the biscuits and mix well.

4 Press the mixture into the tin and press down firmly. Leave to chill in the fridge for about 6 hours, until set quite firm.

5 Cut into 16 squares and store in an airtight tin.

# MARSHMALLOW SLICES

*When the children are home from school on holiday and are fed up with amusing themselves, get them doing some cooking! They love to have something to show for their time and effort.*

**MAKES 16**
100g (4 oz) butter
3 tbsp golden syrup
25g (1 oz) drinking chocolate
225g (8 oz) digestive biscuits, crumbled
50g (2 oz) marshmallows, snipped into small pieces with wet scissors

*For the topping*
125g (4½ oz) Bournville chocolate, melted

1 Wet a 17.5cm (7 in) square cake tin and line with cling film.

2 Measure the butter, syrup and drinking chocolate into a large pan over a low heat and stir gently until the butter has melted.

3 Remove from the heat and allow to cool slightly before stirring in the biscuits and marshmallows. Mix well until thoroughly blended.

4 Turn the mixture into the tin and level the top. Press down firmly with the back of a spoon then leave to chill in the fridge for about 6 hours, until firm.

5 Spread this biscuit base with the melted chocolate, then leave for another hour to set.

6 Peel off the cling film and cut into squares to serve.

# CHOCOLATE CHIP BARS

*These crunchy bars are a hot favourite in our house. They are very easy to make because everything is put in one bowl.*

**MAKES 16**

100g (4 oz) butter, softened
150g (5 oz) demerara sugar
1 large egg
1 tsp vanilla extract
225g (8 oz) self-raising flour
100g (4 oz) chocolate chips

1 Preheat the oven to 190°C/Fan 170°C/Gas 5 and grease a 27.5 x 17.5cm (11 x 7 in) Swiss roll tin.

2 Measure all the ingredients into a bowl and mix thoroughly. If you find it easier, use your hands.

3 Spread the mixture into the tin and bake in the preheated oven for 35–40 minutes, until golden brown and shrinking slightly from the sides of the tin.

4 Leave to cool slightly then cut into 16 pieces.

5 Lift out and leave to finish cooling on a wire rack.

# CHOCOLATE KRISPIES

*Make sure the Krispies are mixed really well so that they are thoroughly coated with the chocolate mixture.*

**MAKES 15**
100g (4 oz) butter
3 rounded tbsp golden syrup
1 level tbsp cocoa powder
25g (1 oz) Bournville chocolate
75g (3 oz) Rice Krispies

**1** Arrange 15 fairy cake paper cases on a large baking sheet.

**2** Melt the butter and syrup in a small pan over a gentle heat. Add the cocoa and chocolate. Remove from the heat and stir until melted.

**3** Add the Krispies and mix very thoroughly until they are well coated.

**4** Spoon into the paper cases and leave to harden in a cool room for about 1 hour.

# TOFFEE AND CHOCOLATE KRISPIE SQUARES

*These are delicious. They take a little time to make but are really worth the effort.*

**MAKES 16**

75g (3 oz) butter
150g (5 oz) granulated
    sugar
1 tbsp golden syrup
1 x 397g can full-fat
    condensed milk
100g (4 oz) Rice Krispies

*For the topping*
100g (4 oz) Bournville
    chocolate, melted

1 Lightly grease a 17.5cm (7 in) square cake tin and line with non-stick baking paper.

2 Measure the butter, sugar, golden syrup and condensed milk into a thick-based pan and heat gently until the sugar has dissolved and the butter has melted. Bring slowly to the boil and simmer for 20 minutes, until thick and a rich caramel colour. Stir continuously and scrape the bottom and sides of the pan, otherwise the mixture will catch.

3 Remove from the heat and drop a little of the mixture into cold water. If it hardens it is ready. Stir in the Rice Krispies to coat them well.

4 Tip the mixture into the tin and pack down. Work quickly as it will harden.

5 Pour over the melted chocolate and spread to cover completely.

6 Leave to cool until set.

7 When cold, cut into 16 squares and store in an airtight container.

# CHOCOLATE AND SULTANA CLUSTERS

*These are most children's all-time favourites. For best results they should be eaten on the day they are made – this is usually no problem! Let the children make them themselves and try to persuade them that it is worth waiting for the clusters to set.*

**MAKES 12**
50g (2 oz) butter
1 rounded tbsp golden syrup
75g (3 oz) Bournville chocolate, broken into pieces
75g (3 oz) cornflakes
50g (2 oz) sultanas

1 Arrange 12 fairy cake paper cases on a large baking sheet.

2 Measure the butter and syrup into a saucepan and heat gently until melted.

3 Remove from the heat and stir in the chocolate. Mix well until melted.

4 Tip in all the cornflakes and sultanas and stir very well so they become evenly coated with the chocolate mixture.

5 Using two spoons, pile the mixture into the paper cases and then leave to harden in a cool room for about 30 minutes.

# ANNABEL'S CARAMEL BARS

*Children love to eat these bars instead of cakes or biscuits; I find they are also very popular accompaniments to ice cream. You can cut down the recipe and make only half the quantity, but in our house they are so popular and useful that it never seems worthwhile making less.*

**MAKES 21**
100g (4 oz) butter
100g (4 oz)
   marshmallows
100g (4 oz) toffees
200g (7 oz) Rice Krispies

**1** You will need a 30 x 23cm (12 x 9 in) traybake tin.

**2** Measure the butter, marshmallows and toffees into a pan and heat gently over a moderate heat until melted and smooth. Be patient, this will take about 5 minutes.

**3** Meanwhile, measure the Krispies into a large bowl.

**4** Remove the pan from the heat and pour all at once on to the Krispies. Stir very thoroughly until they are evenly coated.

**5** Spoon into the tin and press flat with the back of a spoon. Leave in a cool place for about 1–2 hours until set.

**6** Cut into 21 bars.

# HAPPY FACE BISCUITS

*This biscuit recipe can be used in a variety of ways – use different shapes or add your own flavourings.*

**MAKES ABOUT 24**

175g (6 oz) butter, softened
100g (4 oz) caster sugar, plus extra to sprinkle
finely grated zest of 1 lemon
2 large egg yolks, plus a little egg white to glaze
225g (8 oz) plain flour
about 100g (4 oz) currants

1 Cream the butter with the sugar until light and fluffy. Gradually work in the lemon zest, egg yolks and flour. Knead until smooth then wrap in cling film and leave to chill in the fridge for about 1 hour, until firm.

2 Preheat the oven to 180°C/Fan 160°C/Gas 4 and line two large baking sheets with non-stick baking paper.

3 Roll out the dough to 3mm (1/8 in) thickness and cut into rounds with a 7.5cm (3 in) cutter.

4 Arrange the biscuits on the prepared baking sheets and use the currants to make a happy face on each one. Brush with a little egg white, sprinkle with a little caster sugar and bake in the preheated oven for about 12–15 minutes until pale golden brown.

5 Leave to cool on the sheets for a few moments then lift off with a palette knife and finish cooling on a wire rack.

# COCONUT ICE

*This is an easy, no-cook recipe that children can make on their own.*

**MAKES 36**

12 tbsp full-fat
   condensed milk
350g (12 oz) icing sugar
175g (6 oz) desiccated
   coconut
a few drops red
   colouring

1 Lightly grease a 17.5cm (7 in) square tin.

2 Measure the condensed milk, icing sugar and coconut together into a large bowl and mix very thoroughly until the mixture comes together and can be lightly kneaded to a smooth ball.

3 Press half of the mixture evenly over the base of the tin.

4 Add some red colouring to the remaining mixture in the bowl. It is surprising how much will be needed to make a good pink colour – the best way to add the colour is to drip it, drop by drop, from a skewer dipped in the red colouring. Work each addition thoroughly into the mixture to make sure that the pink is a good colour throughout.

5 Press the pink mixture on top of the white mixture and leave in a cool place to set for 1–2 hours, but preferably overnight.

6 Cut into 36 squares and store in an airtight tin.

# COCONUT CRACKERJACKS

*These are similar to flapjacks but the addition of coconut gives a crisp texture that is always popular.*

**MAKES 18**
150g (5 oz) baking spread, from fridge
150g (5 oz) demerara sugar
150g (5 oz) rolled oats
25g (1 oz) desiccated coconut

1 Preheat the oven to 160°C/Fan 140°C/Gas 3 and grease a 27.5 x 17.5 cm (11 x 7 in) Swiss roll tin.

2 Cream the spread and sugar together then add the oats and coconut and work the mixture together.

3 Press this into the tin and bake in the preheated oven for 40–45 minutes, until golden brown.

4 Leave to cool in the tin for about 10 minutes then mark into 18 squares or fingers. Finish cooling in the tin.

5 Lift out and store in an airtight container.

# SULTANA FLAPJACKS

*These are simple and quick to make from ingredients that are in the store cupboard. Most children find them very easy both to make and eat!*

**MAKES 16**
175g (6 oz) butter
125g (4½ oz) demerara sugar
50g (2 oz) golden syrup
200g (7 oz) rolled oats
75g (3 oz) sultanas

1 Preheat the oven to 180°C/Fan 160°C/Gas 4. Grease a 17.5cm (7 in) shallow square tin and line with non-stick baking paper.

2 Measure the butter, sugar and syrup into a small pan and heat gently over a low heat until the butter has melted.

3 Remove from the heat and stir in the oats and sultanas. Mix well then turn into the tin and press flat.

4 Bake in the preheated oven for 30–35 minutes, or until pale golden brown.

5 Remove from the oven and leave for 10 minutes. Mark into 16 fingers then leave to finish cooling in the tin.

6 Lift out and store in an airtight container.

# CHEWY ALMOND FLAPJACKS

*A very dear lady in the village gave me this recipe. I tried it at home and it went down a treat with the family.*

**MAKES 16**

200g (7 oz) butter
200g (7 oz) golden syrup
100g (4 oz) demerara sugar
200g (7 oz) porridge oats
100g (4 oz) flaked almonds

1 Preheat the oven to 180°C/Fan 160°C/Gas 4. Grease a 17.5cm (7 in) square tin and line with non-stick baking paper.

2 Measure the butter, syrup and sugar into a small pan and heat gently over a low heat until the butter has melted.

3 Measure the oats and flaked almonds into a large bowl and pour the melted mixture over the top. Stir well until thoroughly mixed.

4 Spread evenly into the tin and bake in the preheated oven for 30–35 minutes, or until golden brown.

5 Remove from the oven and mark into 16 squares. Leave to cool in the tin.

6 Lift out and store in an airtight tin.

# ORANGE MARSHMALLOW CAKE

*Marshmallows give a lovely topping to this cake. Arrange them on the top as soon as it comes out of the oven so that they soften and stick to the cake then, when cold, pour over the icing.*

**SERVES 8**
100g (4 oz) baking
   spread, from fridge
100g (4 oz) caster sugar
100g (4 oz) self-raising
   flour
½ level tsp baking
   powder
2 large eggs
finely grated zest
   of 1 orange

*For the topping*
about 75g (3 oz) mini
   marshmallows

*For the icing*
175g (6 oz) icing sugar,
   sifted
about 3 tbsp orange
   juice, warmed

1 Preheat the oven to 180°C/Fan 160°C/Gas 4. Grease a 20cm (8 in) loose-bottomed cake or springform tin and line with non-stick baking paper.

2 Measure all the cake ingredients into a bowl and beat with an electric mixer until light, fluffy and well blended.

3 Turn the mixture into the tin, level the top and bake in the preheated oven for 20–25 minutes, or until well risen and golden brown. The cake will have shrunk slightly from the sides of the tin and the top will spring back when pressed with a finger.

4 Remove the cake from the oven and place the marshmallows over the top. Leave to cool in the tin.

5 Meanwhile, blend the icing sugar and orange juice together.

6 Lift the cake from the tin, remove the paper and place on a serving plate. Pour the icing over the top just before serving – the icing will run away into any cracks in the marshmallow topping and slightly down the sides.

# JAMMY BUNS

*I asked a 12-year-old girl to try this recipe for me – she had no problems and thoroughly enjoyed herself. The buns are best eaten fresh from the oven.*

**MAKES 12**
225g (8 oz) self-raising flour
¼ level tsp ground mixed spice
50g (2 oz) butter
50g (2 oz) caster sugar
1 large egg, beaten
about 2 tbsp milk
about 2 tbsp strawberry jam
a little granulated sugar

**1** Preheat the oven to 200°C/Fan 180°C/Gas 6 and line a large baking sheet with non-stick baking paper.

**2** Measure the flour and spice into a bowl and rub in the butter until the mixture resembles fine breadcrumbs. Stir in the sugar.

**3** Blend the egg with the milk then stir into the mixture, adding sufficient liquid to make a stiff dough.

**4** Divide into 12 pieces and roll into balls. Make a hole in the centre of each ball with the handle of a wooden spoon – wiggle it about a bit to make the hole as big as possible. Measure about ½ teaspoon of jam into each hole then pinch the opening firmly to close together.

**5** Turn the buns over and place them, sealed side down, on the baking sheets. Sprinkle with a little granulated sugar and bake in the preheated oven for 10–15 minutes, or until pale golden brown.

**6** Lift off with a palette knife and place on a wire rack. Serve warm.

# BAKED ALASKA BIRTHDAY CAKE

*When I made this for Annabel's birthday cake a few years ago, instead of candles I served it with a sparkler burning in the top. She and all her friends thought it was wonderful.*

**SERVES 8**

1 Swiss Roll
   (shop-bought
   or see page 36)
about 8 scoops
   raspberry ripple
   ice cream (not the
   soft-scoop type)
4 large egg whites
200g (7 oz) caster sugar

**1** Cut the Swiss roll into 8 slices and arrange in a round on an ovenproof plate. Pile the scoops of ice-cream on top of the Swiss roll and put in the freezer whilst making the meringue.

**2** Place the egg whites in a large bowl and whisk on high speed with an electric mixer until they form soft peaks.

**3** Add the sugar, a generous dessertspoonful at a time, whisking well after each addition, until all the sugar has been added.

**4** Take the cake from the freezer and spread the meringue all over so that the ice cream is completely sealed inside. Return to the freezer until required. It will keep in the freezer at this stage for up to 1 week.

**5** To serve, heat the oven to 230°C/Fan 210°C/Gas 8 and bake the cake for about 3 minutes until just tinged golden brown. Serve at once.

# CHAPTER EIGHT
# TEA BREADS AND SCONES

# FARMHOUSE FRUIT LOAF

*A fruit cake baked in a loaf tin – very easy to cut for serving and packing in a lunch box.*

**SERVES 10**

225g (8 oz) self-raising flour
50g (2 oz) glacé cherries, quartered, rinsed and thoroughly dried
175g (6 oz) baking spread or softened butter
175g (6 oz) light muscovado sugar
3 large eggs
2 tbsp milk
175g (6 oz) seedless raisins
175g (6 oz) sultanas

**1** Preheat the oven to 160°C/Fan 140°C/Gas 3. Grease a 900g (2 lb) loaf tin and line with non-stick baking paper.

**2** Measure all the ingredients into a bowl and beat thoroughly until well blended.

**3** Turn the mixture into the tin, level the top and bake in the preheated oven for about 2 hours, or until a skewer inserted into the centre of the loaf comes out clean.

**4** Leave to cool in the tin for 10 minutes then turn out and finish cooling on a wire rack.

FAST CAKES
276
TEA
BREADS
AND
SCONES

# FRUIT MALT LOAF

*This loaf is so easy (and so good) that I am sure children could make it. All the ingredients are likely to be to hand in the store cupboard. Serve the loaf sliced, spread with butter.*

**SERVES 8–10**

175g (6 oz) self-raising flour
2 level tbsp Ovaltine malt drink powder
25g (1 oz) caster or light muscovado sugar
75g (3 oz) sultanas
2 tbsp golden syrup
150ml (¼ pint) milk

1 Preheat the oven to 180°C/Fan 160°C/Gas 4. Grease a 450g (1 lb) loaf tin and line with non-stick baking paper.

2 Measure all the ingredients into a large bowl and beat thoroughly until well blended.

3 Turn the mixture into the tin and bake in the preheated oven for 50–60 minutes, or until a skewer inserted into the centre of the loaf comes out clean.

4 Turn out and leave to cool on a wire rack.

FAST CAKES
277
TEA
BREADS
AND
SCONES

# OLD ENGLISH SEED CAKE

*Seed cakes were always popular in the past; this one is a more updated version.*

**SERVES 8**

175g (6 oz) baking
    spread, from fridge
100g (4 oz) caster sugar
2 large eggs
225g (8 oz) self-raising
    flour
1 level tsp baking
    powder
1 rounded tbsp caraway
    seeds
finely grated zest
    of 1 lemon
4 tbsp milk

**1** Preheat the oven to 180°C/Fan 160°C/Gas 4. Grease a 17.5cm (7 in) deep round cake tin and line with non-stick baking paper.

**2** Measure all the ingredients into a bowl and beat with an electric mixer until well blended.

**3** Turn the mixture into the tin, level the top and bake in the preheated oven for about 1 hour, until well risen and shrinking from the sides of the tin. A skewer inserted into the centre of the cake should come out clean.

**4** Leave to cool in the tin for about 10 minutes then turn out, remove the paper and finish cooling on a wire rack.

FAST CAKES
278
TEA
BREADS
AND
SCONES

# YORKSHIRE TEA BREAD

*This tea bread is quick to make and will keep for up to two weeks in an airtight tin. Serve sliced, spread with unsalted butter.*

**SERVES 10**

225g (8 oz) mixed dried fruit

175ml (6 fl oz) cold strained tea

100g (4 oz) dark soft brown sugar

225g (8 oz) self-raising flour

2 large eggs

1 Soak the mixed fruit overnight in the tea in a large bowl, covered with a plate. If this is not possible, put the fruit in hot tea and leave for several hours, until the fruit soaks up most of the liquid.

2 Preheat the oven to 160°C/Fan 140°C/Gas 3. Grease a 900g (2 lb) loaf tin and line with non-stick baking paper.

3 Add the remaining ingredients to the fruit and beat until well blended.

4 Pour into the tin and bake in the preheated oven for about 1 hour, or until a skewer inserted into the centre of the tea bread comes out clean.

5 Leave to cool in the tin then turn out and finish cooling on a wire rack.

FAST CAKES
281
TEA
BREADS
AND
SCONES

# HONEY LOAF

*This loaf is very good if it is served thinly sliced and spread with unsalted butter.*

**SERVES 12**

50g (2 oz) mixed peel
350g (12 oz) self-raising flour
1 level tbsp ground mixed spice
100g (4 oz) soft brown sugar
175g (6 oz) clear honey
150ml (¼ pint) milk
25g (1 oz) sugar lumps, crushed

1 Preheat the oven to 180°C/Fan 160°C/Gas 4. Grease a 900g (2 lb) loaf tin and line with non-stick baking paper.

2 Chop the peel very finely and place in a bowl with the flour, spice and brown sugar and stir until well blended. Make a well in the centre, stir in the honey and milk and blend until a smooth, stiff dough is formed.

3 Turn into the tin, sprinkle the crushed sugar lumps over the top of the loaf then bake in the preheated oven for about 1¼ hours. The loaf should be shrinking from the sides of the tin and a skewer inserted into the centre should come out clean.

4 Turn out, remove the paper and leave to cool on a wire rack.

FAST CAKES
282
TEA
BREADS
AND
SCONES

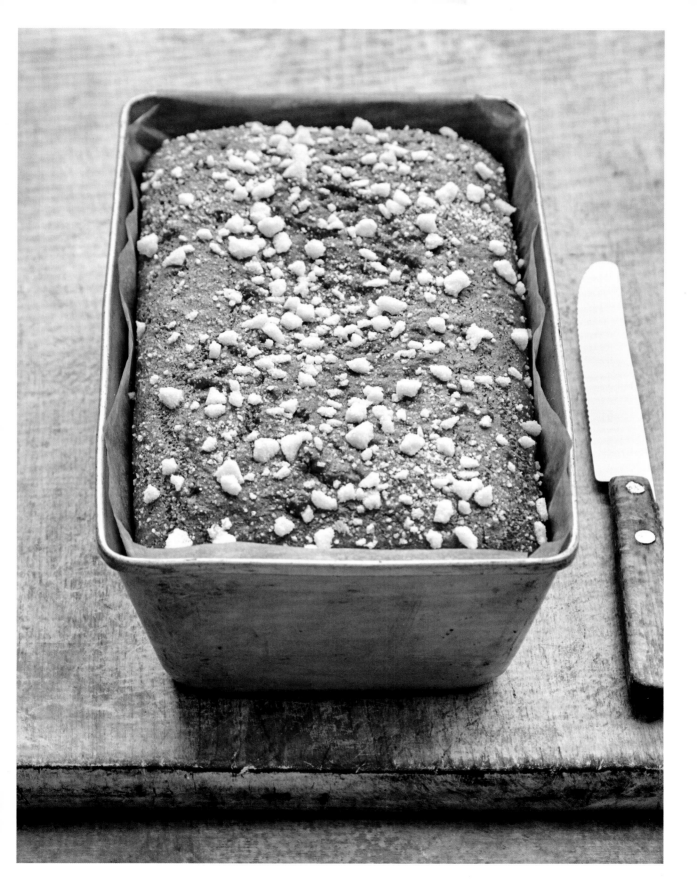

# ORANGE AND WALNUT LOAF

*Serve this loaf in slices, alone or spread with butter. For a change add currants instead of the candied peel, and lemon zest and juice instead of the orange. Both combinations are delicious.*

## SERVES 8–10

175g (6 oz) self-raising flour
¾ level tsp baking powder
finely grated zest and juice of 1 large orange
50g (2 oz) walnuts, chopped
50g (2 oz) candied peel, chopped
75g (3 oz) baking spread, from fridge
75g (3 oz) light muscovado sugar
1 large egg, beaten
3 tbsp milk

1 Preheat the oven to 180°C/Fan 160°C/Gas 4. Grease a 450g (1 lb) loaf tin and line with non-stick baking paper.

2 Measure all the ingredients into a large bowl and beat well until thoroughly blended.

3 Turn into the tin and bake in the preheated oven for about 1 hour, or until well risen. A skewer inserted into the centre of the loaf should come out clean.

4 Leave to cool in the tin for about 15 minutes then turn out, remove the paper and finish cooling on a wire rack.

FAST CAKES
284
TEA
BREADS
AND
SCONES

# MILD GINGER LOAF

*This is very easy to make. I often have stem ginger left on the shelf after Christmas, and this is one of my favourite ways of using it up. Best to eat within 2 days of baking. This is lovely served in slices with butter.*

**SERVES 10–12**

100g (4 oz) baking spread, from fridge

100g (4 oz) light muscovado sugar

2 tbsp black treacle

225g (8 oz) self-raising flour

1 level tsp baking powder

1 level tsp ground ginger

50g (2 oz) stem ginger, well drained and chopped

2 large eggs

1 Preheat the oven to 160°C/Fan 140°C/Gas 3. Grease a 900g (2 lb) loaf tin and line with non-stick baking paper.

2 Measure the baking spread, sugar and treacle into a pan and heat gently until the spread has melted.

3 Put all the dry ingredients in a mixing bowl, add the melted mixture, the chopped ginger and eggs and beat well for a minute until thoroughly blended.

4 Pour into the tin and bake in the preheated oven for about 45 minutes, or until well risen. A skewer inserted into the centre of the loaf should come out clean.

5 Leave to cool in the tin for about 5 minutes then turn out, remove the paper and finish cooling on a wire rack.

# TACKY GINGERBREAD

*Chopped stem ginger gives this gingerbread a very special flavour and the finished cake looks delicious if it is iced with a simple lemon icing and decorated with small pieces of crystallised lemon.*

**MAKES 12 SQUARES**

175g (6 oz) plain flour
¾ level tsp baking powder
2 level tsp ground ginger
50g (2 oz) baking spread, from fridge
50g (2 oz) light muscovado sugar
1 tbsp black treacle
1 tbsp golden syrup
1 level tsp bicarbonate of soda
210ml (7 fl oz) warm milk
2 large eggs
40g (1½ oz) stem ginger, finely chopped

**1** Preheat the oven to 160°C/Fan 140°C/Gas 3. Grease a 20cm (8 in) square cake tin and line with non-stick baking paper.

**2** Sift the flour, baking powder and ground ginger into a bowl.

**3** Cream the spread and sugar together with the treacle and syrup in a large bowl and beat very well.

**4** Dissolve the bicarbonate of soda in the warm milk then stir into the creamed sugary mixture. Add the flour mixture, the eggs and stem ginger and beat well until thoroughly blended.

**5** Turn into the tin and bake in the preheated oven for about 45 minutes, or until the gingerbread is risen and firm to the touch.

**6** Leave to cool in the tin.

FAST CAKES
287
TEA
BREADS
AND
SCONES

# CHOCOLATE AND ORANGE LOAF

*This is quite a shallow loaf but is beautifully moist and can be eaten happily without any butter.*

**SERVES 10–12**

175g (6 oz) baking spread, from fridge
175g (6 oz) caster sugar
175g (6 oz) self-raising flour
¾ level tsp baking powder
finely grated zest of 1 orange
3 large eggs
2 tbsp milk

*For the icing*
50g (2 oz) butter
25g (1 oz) cocoa powder, sifted
2–3 tbsp orange juice
100g (4 oz) icing sugar, sifted

1 Preheat the oven to 190°C/Fan 170°C/Gas 5. Grease a 900g (2 lb) loaf tin and line with non-stick baking paper.

2 Measure all the ingredients for the loaf into a large mixing bowl and beat with an electric mixer until well blended.

3 Turn the mixture into the tin and bake in the preheated oven for about 1 hour until well risen and the top springs back when lightly pressed with a finger.

4 Leave to cool in the tin then turn out and remove the paper.

5 To make the icing, measure the butter, cocoa, orange juice and icing sugar into a bowl. Beat well to a light, smooth consistency.

6 Spread the icing evenly over the top of the loaf and serve in slices.

FAST CAKES
288
TEA
BREADS
AND
SCONES

# ROUND ORANGE TEA BREAD

*A simple tea bread with a lovely orange flavour. Prepare it in the afternoon with the remains of the tea, leave to stand overnight and then make the bread the following morning.*

**SERVES 10**

150g (5 oz) currants
150g (5 oz) seedless raisins
150g (5 oz) light muscovado sugar
finely grated zest of 2 oranges
300ml (½ pint) hot tea
275g (10 oz) self-raising flour
1 large egg, beaten

1 Put the fruit, sugar and orange zest in a bowl and pour in the hot tea. Stir very well, cover with a plate to keep the heat in and then leave to stand overnight.

2 Preheat the oven to 150°C/Fan 130°C/Gas 2. Grease a 20cm (8 in) round cake tin and line with non-stick baking paper.

3 Stir the flour and egg into the soaked fruit and mix very well.

4 Turn the mixture into the tin and bake in the preheated oven for about 1½ hours, or until the tea bread is shrinking from the sides of the tin. A skewer inserted into the centre should come out clean.

5 Turn out, remove the paper and leave to cool on a wire rack.

6 Serve sliced, either spread with butter or just as it is.

FAST CAKES
290
TEA
BREADS
AND
SCONES

# ALL-BRAN TEA BREAD LOAF

*Soak the fruit overnight so that it plumps up and the next day all that is necessary is to stir the remaining ingredients into the mixture. It is a very easy loaf to make and the finished result has a lovely flavour. Serve sliced and spread with butter or just as it is.*

**SERVES 10**

350g (12 oz) mixed
   dried fruit
225g (8 oz) demerara
   sugar
300ml (½ pint) cold tea
150g (5 oz) self-raising
   flour
150g (5 oz) All-Bran
1 large egg, beaten

**1** Put the fruit and sugar in a bowl and pour over the tea. Stir well then leave to stand overnight.

**2** Preheat the oven to 150°C/Fan 130°C/Gas 2. Grease a 900g (2 lb) loaf tin and line with non-stick baking paper.

**3** Stir the flour, All-Bran and egg into the fruit and mix very thoroughly.

**4** Turn the mixture into the tin and bake in the preheated oven for about 2 hours, or until the mixture has risen slightly and shrinks away from the sides of the tin. A skewer inserted into the centre should come out clean.

**5** Turn out and leave to cool on a wire rack.

FAST CAKES
291
TEA
BREADS
AND
SCONES

# QUICK CHERRY LOAF

*Be sure to wash and dry the glacé cherries thoroughly otherwise they do have a tendency to sink!*

**SERVES 8–10**

100g (4 oz) glacé cherries, chopped, rinsed and thoroughly dried
100g (4 oz) self-raising flour
100g (4 oz) baking spread, from fridge
100g (4 oz) caster sugar
2 large eggs
finely grated zest of 1 small orange
25g (1 oz) semolina

1 Preheat the oven to 180°C/Fan 160°C/Gas 4. Grease a 450g (1 lb) loaf tin and line with non-stick baking paper.

2 Measure all the ingredients into a large bowl and beat well until thoroughly blended.

3 Turn the mixture into the tin, level the top and bake in the preheated oven for about 40–45 minutes, or until well risen. A skewer inserted into the centre of the loaf should come out clean.

4 Leave to cool in the tin for a few minutes then turn out, remove the paper and finish cooling on a wire rack.

5 Serve in slices.

FAST CAKES
292
TEA
BREADS
AND
SCONES

# BANANA LOAF

*A delicious cut-and-come-again loaf that really tastes of banana.*

**SERVES 10**

2 ripe bananas, mashed down with a fork
100g (4 oz) wholemeal flour
150g (5 oz) self-raising flour
1 level tsp baking powder
100g (4 oz) baking spread, from fridge
175g (6 oz) light muscovado sugar
2 large eggs
1 x 150g pot natural yoghurt
150g (5 oz) currants
2 tbsp milk

1 Preheat the oven to 180°C/Fan 160°C/Gas 4. Grease a 900g (2 lb) loaf tin and line with non-stick baking paper.

2 Measure all the ingredients into a large mixing bowl and beat well until thoroughly blended.

3 Turn into the tin and bake in the preheated oven for about 1½ hours, or until well risen. A skewer inserted into the centre of the loaf should come out clean.

4 Leave to cool in the tin for about 15 minutes then turn out, remove the paper and finish cooling on a wire rack.

5 Serve in slices with butter.

FAST CAKES
294
TEA
BREADS
AND
SCONES

# NORTH-COUNTRY PARKIN

*Store for at least a week before eating in order to allow time for the treacly flavour to develop fully.*

**MAKES 16 PIECES**

350g (12 oz) medium oatmeal
175g (6 oz) plain flour
1 level tbsp caster sugar
½ level tsp ground ginger
100g (4 oz) baking spread, from fridge
450g (1 lb) black treacle
5 tbsp milk
½ level tsp bicarbonate of soda

**1** Preheat the oven to 190°C/Fan 170°C/Gas 5. Grease the base of a 30 x 23cm (12 x 9 in) traybake tin and line with non-stick baking paper.

**2** Measure the oatmeal, flour, sugar and ginger into a large bowl.

**3** Measure the spread and treacle into a pan and heat gently until the spread has melted.

**4** Warm the milk in a separate pan and stir in the bicarbonate of soda until dissolved. Add to the treacle mixture.

**5** Make a well in the centre of the dry ingredients and stir in the wet ingredients. Mix very well until thoroughly blended.

**6** Turn the mixture into the tin and bake in the preheated oven for about 40 minutes, or until the parkin is shrinking away from the sides of the tin. A skewer inserted into the centre of the parkin should come out clean.

**7** Turn out and leave to cool on a wire rack.

**8** When quite cold cut into 16 pieces. Store for a week before serving.

FAST CAKES
295
TEA
BREADS
AND
SCONES

# WELSH CURRANT LOAF

*This loaf lasts extremely well, especially if kept wrapped in cling film.*

**SERVES 10–12**

175g (6 oz) currants
175g (6 oz) sultanas
225g (8 oz) light
    muscovado sugar
300ml (½ pint) cider
150g (5 oz) self-raising
    flour
150g (5 oz) wholemeal
    flour
1 level tsp baking
    powder
1 large egg, beaten

**1** Measure the fruits and sugar into a large mixing bowl, pour over the cider and leave to stand overnight covered with cling film.

**2** Preheat the oven to 150°C/Fan 130°C/Gas 2. Grease a 900g (2 lb) loaf tin and line with non-stick baking paper.

**3** Stir the flours, baking powder and egg into the fruit mixture and beat well until thoroughly blended.

**4** Turn the mixture into the tin and level the top. Bake in the preheated oven for about 1¾ hours, or until well risen. A skewer inserted into the centre of the loaf should come out clean.

**5** Leave to cool in the tin for a few minutes then turn out, remove the paper and finish cooling on a wire rack.

**6** Serve in slices spread with butter.

FAST CAKES
296
TEA
BREADS
AND
SCONES

# CLASSIC SPECIAL SCONES

*The secret of a good scone is not to have the mixture too dry and not to handle the dough too much.*

**MAKES 10**
225g (8 oz) self-raising
    flour
1 level tsp baking
    powder
50g (2 oz) butter
25g (1 oz) caster sugar
1 large egg
milk

**1** Preheat the oven to 220°C/Fan 200°C/Gas 7 and lightly grease a baking sheet.

**2** Measure the flour and baking powder into a bowl, add the butter and rub in until the mixture resembles fine breadcrumbs. Stir in the sugar.

**3** Crack the egg into a measuring jug, lightly beat then make up to 125ml (4 fl oz) with the milk. Stir most of the egg and milk into the flour, keeping 1 tablespoon in the jug to glaze the scones before baking. Mix to a soft dough.

**4** Turn on to a lightly floured surface, knead lightly then roll out to 1.25cm (½ in) thickness. Cut into rounds with a fluted 8cm (3 in) cutter to make 10 scones.

**5** Place the scones, spaced, on the baking sheet. Brush the tops with the remaining egg and milk mixture and bake in the preheated oven for about 10 minutes, or until a pale golden brown.

**6** Remove from the baking sheet and leave to cool on a wire rack.

**VARIATION: GOLDEN SCONES**
Use light muscovado sugar instead of caster and add 1 tablespoon of golden syrup to the milk and egg mixture. Beat thoroughly to blend before adding to the flour mixture.

FAST CAKES
298
TEA
BREADS
AND
SCONES

# WHOLEMEAL SCONES

*The wholemeal flour makes a healthy addition – all the more reason to serve with clotted cream and jam!*

**MAKES 10**

125g (4½ oz) self-raising flour
100g (4 oz) wholemeal flour
1 rounded tsp baking powder
50g (2 oz) butter
25g (1 oz) caster sugar
1 large egg
milk

1 Preheat the oven to 220°C/Fan 200°C/Gas 7 and lightly grease a baking sheet.

2 Put the flours and baking powder in a bowl, add the butter and rub in until the mixture resembles fine breadcrumbs. Stir in the sugar.

3 Crack the egg into a measuring jug, lightly beat then make up to 150ml (¼ pint) with milk. Stir most of the egg and milk into the flour, keeping 1 tablespoon in the jug to glaze the scones before baking. Mix to a soft dough.

4 Turn on to a lightly floured surface, knead lightly then roll out to 1.25cm (½ in) thickness. Cut into rounds with a fluted 8cm (3 in) cutter to make 10 scones.

5 Place the scones, spaced, on the baking sheet. Brush the tops with the remaining egg and milk mixture and bake in the preheated oven for about 10 minutes, or until a pale golden brown.

6 Remove the scones from the baking sheet and leave to cool on a wire rack.

**VARIATION: FRUIT SCONES**
Add 50–75g (2–3 oz) dried mixed fruit to the rubbed-in mixture.

FAST CAKES
300
TEA
BREADS
AND
SCONES

# CHEESE SCONES

*Wrapping scones in a tea towel after baking helps to keep them moist.*

**MAKES 10**
225g (8 oz) self-raising
 flour
1 level tsp dry mustard
¼ level tsp salt
good pinch of cayenne
 pepper
1 level tsp baking
 powder
50g (2 oz) butter
100g (4 oz) finely
 grated cheese
1 large egg
milk

**1** Preheat the oven to 220°C/Fan 200°C/Gas 7 and lightly grease a baking sheet.

**2** Measure the flour, mustard, salt, cayenne and baking powder into a bowl. Add the butter and rub in until the mixture resembles fine breadcrumbs. Stir in the cheese.

**3** Crack the egg into a measuring jug, lightly beat it and then make up to 150ml (¼ pint) with milk. Stir most of the egg and milk into the flour, keeping 1 tablespoon in the jug to glaze the scones before baking. Mix to a soft dough.

**4** Turn on to a lightly floured surface, knead lightly then roll out to 1.25cm (½ in) thickness. Cut into rounds with a fluted 8cm (3 in) cutter to make 10 scones.

**5** Place the scones, spaced, on the baking sheet. Brush the tops with the remaining egg and milk mixture and bake in the preheated oven for about 10 minutes, or until a pale golden brown.

**6** Remove from the oven and leave to cool on a wire rack.

FAST CAKES
301
TEA
BREADS
AND
SCONES

# DROP SCONES

*These are simple to make and a great stand-by when unexpected visitors pop in at the weekend.*

**MAKES 24**

175g (6 oz) self-raising
   flour
1 level tsp baking
   powder
40g (1½ oz) caster sugar
1 large egg
200ml (7 fl oz) milk
a little sunflower oil,
   to grease

**1** Measure the flour, baking powder and sugar into a mixing bowl. Make a well in the centre then add the egg and half the milk. Beat well with a whisk to a smooth, thick batter then beat in enough milk to make the consistency of thick pouring cream.

**2** Heat a large non-stick pan and grease with little oil.

**3** Drop the mixture in dessertspoonfuls on to the hot pan over a medium heat, spacing well apart to allow for them to spread. When bubbles appear on the surface, turn the scones over and cook on the other side for a further 30–60 seconds, or until lightly golden brown.

**4** Lift the pancakes on to a wire rack and cover them with a clean tea towel to keep them soft.

**5** Continue cooking until all the batter has been used then serve warm with butter or blueberries and maple syrup.

---

**VARIATION: TREACLE DROP SCONES**
Add 1 tablespoon of black treacle to the basic recipe and cut down the sugar to just 1 teaspoonful. For a change, add ¼ level teaspoon mixed spice to the flour.

FAST CAKES
302
TEA
BREADS
AND
SCONES

# CHEESE DROP SCONES

*A lovely savoury alternative to a sweet drop scone.*

**MAKES 24**

175g (6 oz) self-raising
  flour
1 level tsp baking
  powder
20g (¾ oz) grated
  Parmesan
½ level tsp dry mustard
¼ level tsp salt
1 large egg
200ml (7 fl oz) milk
a little sunflower oil,
  to grease

1 Measure the flour, baking powder, Parmesan, mustard and salt into a mixing bowl. Make a well in the centre then add the egg and half the milk. Beat well with a whisk to a thick batter then beat in enough milk to make the consistency of thick pouring cream.

2 Heat a large non-stick pan and grease with little oil.

3 Drop the mixture in dessertspoonfuls on to the hot pan over a medium heat, spacing well apart to allow for them to spread. When bubbles appear on the surface, turn the scones over and cook on the other side for a further 30–60 seconds, or until lightly golden brown.

4 Lift the pancakes on to a wire rack and cover them with a clean tea towel to keep them soft.

5 Continue cooking until all the batter has been used then serve warm with butter.

FAST CAKES
304
TEA
BREADS
AND
SCONES

# WELSH CAKES

*These are quick to make and may be made on a traditional griddle or in a heavy non-stick frying pan. The cakes are best eaten on the day that they are made.*

**MAKES 12–14**
225g (8 oz) self-raising flour
100g (4 oz) butter
75g (3 oz) caster sugar, plus extra to dust
75g (3 oz) currants
½ level tsp ground mixed spice
1 large egg
1 tbsp milk

1 Measure the flour into a bowl and rub in the butter until the mixture resembles fine breadcrumbs. Add the sugar, currants and spice.

2 Beat the egg with the milk, add this to the flour and currant mixture and mix to a firm dough.

3 Roll out to 5mm (¼ in) thickness and cut into rounds with a plain 7.5cm (3 in) cutter.

4 Heat a griddle or heavy-based frying pan and grease lightly.

5 Cook the Welsh cakes over a low heat for about 3 minutes on each side until golden brown. Do not cook the cakes too fast otherwise the centres will not be cooked through.

6 Leave to cool on a wire rack.

7 Dust with caster sugar and serve.

FAST CAKES
305
TEA
BREADS
AND
SCONES

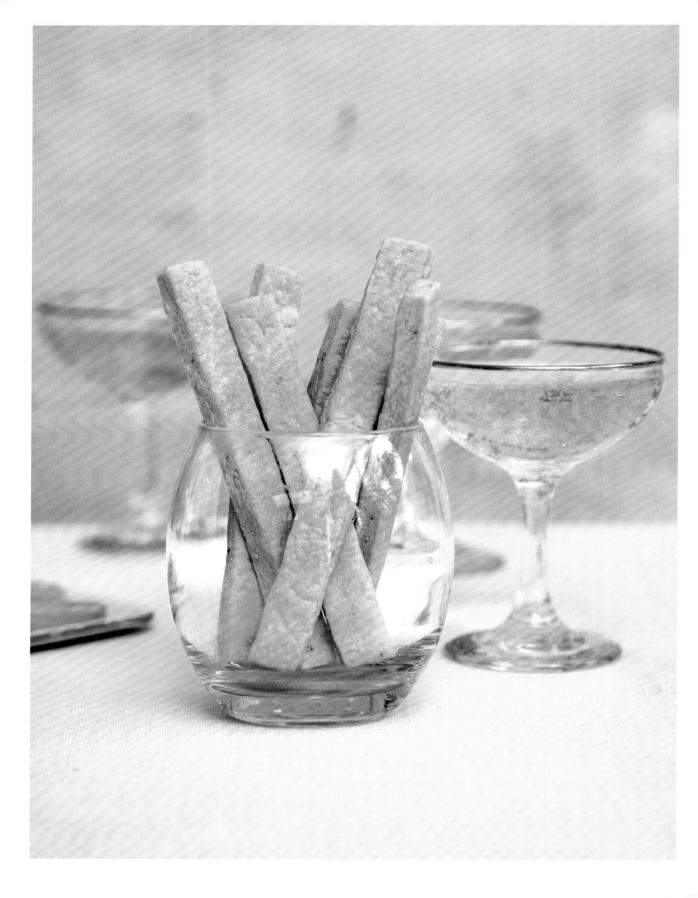

# TRADITIONAL CHEESE STRAWS

*Always popular with those who do not have a particularly sweet tooth, these are good to serve at a drinks party.*

**MAKES 24**
200g (7 oz) self-raising
  flour
1 level tsp mustard
  powder
¼ level tsp salt
freshly ground black
  pepper
100g (4 oz) butter
125g (4½ oz) mature
  Cheddar, grated
a little beaten egg

**1** Preheat the oven to 200°C/Fan 180°C/Gas 6 and lightly grease two or three baking sheets.

**2** Measure the flour, mustard powder, salt and pepper into a bowl and rub in the butter until the mixture resembles fine breadcrumbs. Stir in the cheese, then add sufficient egg to give a firm dough. Turn out on to a lightly floured surface and knead until smooth.

**3** Roll out to 5mm (¼ in) thickness and cut into narrow strips.

**4** Arrange on the baking sheets and bake in the preheated oven for about 10 minutes, or until just beginning to tinge with colour.

**5** Leave to cool on the sheets for a few moments then lift off with a palette knife and finish cooling on a wire rack.

FAST CAKES
307
TEA
BREADS
AND
SCONES

# FAST GRANARY ROLLS

*For lighter rolls, use half granary flour and half strong white flour.*

**MAKES 24**

675g (1½ lb) granary flour

1 x 7g packet fast-action yeast

2 level tsp sea salt, or a little less ordinary salt

1 tbsp sunflower oil

480ml (17 fl oz) hand-hot milk, or milk and water mixed

1 large egg, beaten, to glaze

1 Grease two large baking sheets.

2 Put the plastic dough blade into the food processor then add the dry ingredients and the oil. Process for a few seconds to mix them well then add the liquid in a continuous stream through the feed-tube while the processor is on, to mix to a dough. Process for a further 2 minutes in order to knead the dough.

3 Turn out on to a floured surface. Halve the dough and roll each half into a sausage shape. Divide each one into 12 equal pieces by cutting with a sharp knife. Shape the pieces into rounds by hand and place them, well spaced, on to the baking sheets.

4 Cover the rolls with cling film and put the baking sheets into a warm place to prove for about 1 hour.

5 Preheat the oven to 220°C/Fan 200°C/Gas 7.

6 Once the rolls have doubled in size, glaze with the beaten egg and bake in the preheated oven for about 10–15 minutes, or until they have browned on top and sound hollow when the base is tapped.

7 Cool on a wire rack.

FAST CAKES
308
TEA
BREADS
AND
SCONES

# IRISH SODA BREAD

*If you run out of bread, this is a quick and easy recipe to make. It is best eaten fresh as a tea bread or as a substitute for yeast-baked bread. If you do not have soured milk, fresh milk may be soured by adding 1 tablespoon of lemon juice.*

**MAKES 1 LOAF**

450g (1 lb) plain flour
1 level tsp bicarbonate of soda
1 level tsp salt
50g (2 oz) butter
300ml (½ pint) buttermilk or soured milk

1 Preheat the oven to 220°C/Fan 200°C/Gas 6 and flour a baking sheet.

2 Sift the flour into a bowl with the bicarbonate of soda and salt. Add the butter and rub in until it resembles breadcrumbs.

3 Make a well in the centre and stir in the milk. Mix to a scone-like dough with a round-bladed knife.

4 Turn the dough on to a lightly floured surface and knead lightly. Shape into a 17.5cm (7 in) round and then flatten slightly and place on a floured baking sheet.

5 Mark the round into four with a knife and bake in the preheated oven for about 35 minutes, or until well risen and golden brown.

6 Leave to cool on a wire rack then serve sliced, spread with butter.

FAST CAKES
310
TEA
BREADS
AND
SCONES

# CHEESE AND BRAZIL NUT LOAF

*Make this loaf with whichever nuts you happen to have in the store cupboard.*
*I particularly like it made with Brazil nuts.*

**MAKES 1 LOAF**

100g (4 oz) self-raising flour
100g (4 oz) wholemeal flour
1 level tsp baking powder
1 level tsp dry mustard
1 level tsp salt
freshly ground black pepper
75g (3 oz) butter, softened
100g (4 oz) extra mature Cheddar, grated
50g (2 oz) Brazil nuts, chopped
2 large eggs
150ml (¼ pint) milk

**1** Preheat the oven to 180°C/Fan 160°C/Gas 4. Grease a 450g (1 lb) loaf tin and line with non-stick baking paper.

**2** Measure all the ingredients into a large mixing bowl and beat with an electric mixer until well blended.

**3** Turn the mixture into the tin, level the top and bake in the preheated oven for about 1 hour, or until well risen. A skewer inserted into the centre of the loaf should come out clean.

**4** Leave to cool in the tin for about 5 minutes, then turn out and finish cooling on a wire rack.

FAST CAKES
312
TEA
BREADS
AND
SCONES

# INDEX

# THANK YOUS

This book is a real team effort. Lucy Young has orchestrated the planning of it with her usual expertise and juggling skills!

Jo Roberts Miller, our lovely editor, has brought the book together with beautiful results. Jo is quite exceptional – never have we had an editor who has made so many of the recipes at home for her children! This is the seventh she has edited for us.

Lucinda McCord and Isla Murray have tested the recipes with great dedication. Baking can be tricky when testing recipes and they are the best at making sure the recipes are foolproof for everyone at home.

Muna Reyal, thank you for your idea of bringing this book back to life, and to the team at Headline Home for producing a brilliant book of which I am very proud.

Thank you to Emma and Alex Smith at Smith and Gilmour for the design, Georgia Glynn Smith for the creative photography, home economist Lisa Harrison for being the best and Felicity Bryan – my literary agent of over 40 years.

It has been a joy to bring this book right back up to date and thank you to my special team.